CACTUS

Reaktion's Botanical series is the first of its kind, integrating horticultural and botanical writing with a broader account of the cultural and social impact of trees, plants and flowers.

Cactus

Dan Torre

REAKTION BOOKS

For Lucy, Thomas and Vivienne

Published by
REAKTION BOOKS LTD
Unit 32, Waterside
44–48 Wharf Road
London N1 7UX, UK

www.reaktionbooks.co.uk

First published 2017, reprinted 2018

Printed and bound in China by 1010 Printing International Ltd

A catalogue record for this book is available from the British Library

ISBN 978 1 78023 722 0

Contents

Ernst Heyn, 'Queen of the Night', illustration from Anton Kerner von Marilaun, *Pflanzenleben* (1896).

Introduction

This is the dead land.
This is cactus land.

T. S. ELIOT[1]

People have traditionally regarded the cactus family of plants in contradictory ways, viewing it as both familiar and alien, as both beautiful and menacing. Most individuals have a very definite reaction: they either love cacti or they hate them.

In fact, cacti make up a very diverse group of plants, the family Cactaceae, which comprises approximately 1,500 different species (as well as countless hybrids, cultivars and mutations) – all of which are native exclusively to the Americas. So very diverse is this family that many of its varieties look and behave in vastly different ways. People who claim to dislike them can be surprised when they learn that their favourite hanging plant with the dazzling red and pink flowers is actually a cactus, or are left speechless when they see their first truly amazing display of desert cacti in bloom. Certainly, some cacti do feature rather ferocious-looking spines, and many are indeed well adapted to the harshest and driest of environments; some can look lifeless much of the time. Other cacti look nothing like the stereotypical 'cactus' plant. Some have no spines at all; a few have actual leaves, and some are extremely delicate tropical plants that grow high up among the plants of the rainforest canopy. The saguaro cactus (*Carnegiea gigantea*) can become a towering giant up to 15 m

(50 ft) high that dominates the landscape. *Neobuxbaumia tetezo* of Mexico can grow into such dense forests that the plants are nearly impossible to pass between. Others, such as *Ariocarpus kotschoubeyanus* or *Copiapoa esmeraldana*, reach only a few centimetres in diameter after decades of growth, and are almost never seen at all because they spend most of their life underground. Many cacti exhibit remarkable sculptural structures that could be described as 'more form than foliage', while others are delicate, wispy things that dangle down in sprays of greenery.

Cacti can express hugely contrasting features even within a single plant. They can have some of the most beautiful flowers, and (if one is able to access it) silky-smooth skin; by contrast, they can have some of the most painful of barbed spines. Some cacti can take many years to grow just a few centimetres, and then in a matter of days produce a flower that is substantially larger then the entire plant – and that withers away again after just a day or two. There is incredible variety and contrast to be found in these frequently misunderstood plants, and such variations are the cause of the wavering perceptions people have of the cactus family.

Nearly all cacti are succulent, that is, they have thick, fleshy parts (their stems) that are used to store water; but not all succulent plants are cacti. Succulence is merely a condition or a feature of some plants: it is not a formal classification. Though most cacti are indeed succulent; a few varieties express little or no succulence at all – specifically those belonging to the genus *Pereskia*.

There are a number of other desert plants, such as agaves or the spiny ocotillo shrub (*Fouquieria splendens*, sometimes called the monkey tail cactus or vine cactus), that look rather cactus-like and flourish in the dry desert, but are definitely not part of the family Cactaceae. Another very diverse group of plants, the euphorbias or spurges (Euphorbiaceae), features a number of succulent plants that look almost exactly like cacti. Euphorbias are principally native to the

Opposite: Assorted cacti.

9

Epiphytic (tree-dwelling) cacti (*Rhipsalis* sp.), native to tropical rainforests of South America.

This print from William Woodville's *Medical Botany* (1832) does not show a cactus, but a succulent belonging to the Euphorbiaceae family.

This print from
The Cactaceae (1919)
depicts three
different varieties
of the genus *Pereskia*
– all true cacti that
have leaves and little
or no succulence.

BRITTON AND ROSE   PLATE III

M. E. Eaton del.

1. Flowering branch of *Pereskia grandifolia*.   2. Leafy branch of *Pereskiopsis chapistle*.
3. Leafy branch of *Pereskiopsis pititache*.   (All natural size.)

African continent, and it is really quite extraordinary – and an excellent example of parallel evolution – that plants growing on opposite sides of the world should develop such similar attributes. There are some very distinct differences, though. For example, euphorbias do not have areoles, and their spines and flowers grow directly from their stems; and unlike cacti, most contain a rather toxic sap. Even though there are quite a few features that prove that euphorbias are not cacti, they can easily be mistaken for cacti even by those who are familiar with the plants.

For many years all cacti were illegal in the Australian state of Queensland. This was because of the astonishing outbreak of the introduced prickly pear cactus (*Opuntia* sp.), which invaded vast areas of prime grazing and agricultural land beginning in the late 1800s. Huge amounts of money and effort were expended in combating this

Flowering epiphytic cacti cultivars.

agricultural 'weed', and as a precaution all cacti were banned from being grown in the state. However, as with most regions of the world, there remained a small group of cactus and succulent enthusiasts, known then as the Succulent Society of Queensland. Some members, it was reported, would trade the occasional small potted cacti plant among themselves, and on at least one occasion the authorities raided the members' plant collections, confiscating their cacti. However, not having a precise understanding of the cactus family, they confiscated and destroyed many succulent euphorbias (mistaking them for true cacti), and ignored many of the plants that actually were cacti. Finally, by the 1980s, sentiments were slowly beginning to change. In an effort finally to amend these overly strict laws, several members of the Succulent Society organized a meeting with members of parliament to discuss the matter. They brought with them one of the popular Christmas cacti (*Schlumbergera* sp.). Several of the parliamentarians realized, much to their surprise, that they had an 'illegal cactus' growing in their own homes.[2] Eventually the law was changed, and today only a few varieties of cactus (predominantly the invasive prickly pear) remain illegal. It seems that even governments have had

Collection of cacti in the wild.

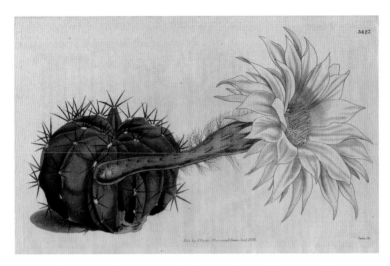

Flowering *Echinopsis* cactus, print from *Curtis's Botanical Magazine*, 1838.

trouble 'putting their finger on' the identity of this somewhat elusive family of plants.

Ultimately, because of the cactus's unique paradoxical attributes and its limited natural geographic origins, it has continually elicited an almost love/hate relationship with humans, who have tended to view it as native or alien, beautiful or beastly, inanimate or very much alive. Few plant families are as complex, as loved and as hated as that of the cactus.

one

Natural History of the Cactus
꧁꧂

C acti are perfectly suited to the desert. They can withstand
scorching heat and little or no rainfall, and have developed
very resourceful means of reproduction and survival. Most
species possess an extraordinary capacity to absorb rapidly any droplet of moisture and to store it efficiently. Many have developed
ingenious ways to protect themselves from the burning sun, including the development of thick protective hair and spines to provide
shade. Some low-lying plants can even pull themselves under the
sand to avoid the direct rays of the sun. Most cacti produce fruit that
contains a vast number of seeds, thus greatly increasing their chances
of germination in their arid habitat. But even more successful are
those cacti that can propagate from stem segments – particularly the
prickly pear and the cholla, the segmented stems of which are easily
detached, and are dispersed by clinging to the fur of animals. When
these segments later fall to the ground, they quickly generate roots
and produce a new plant. This means of propagation has the distinct
advantage that the new plantlet already has substantial reserves of
water stored in its stem, which can ensure its growth for a year or
more without the need for additional moisture. The detached pads
of one Californian prickly pear cactus (*Opuntia basilaris*) can survive
for as long as three years and still be viable for replanting.[1]

Cacti are not limited to desert environments; they can be found
in a variety of climates, from parched wasteland to the dampest
tropics. But the majority do prefer desert-like conditions: a hot,

Saguaro cacti, *Carnegiea gigantea*, in the Sonoran desert, Arizona.

dry climate, with coarse, sandy, well-drained soil. They are adept at absorbing very quickly all moisture with which they come into contact. Because of this, if the soil is not well-drained their roots can be prone to disease and rot. Cacti generally prefer warm temperatures and, although some species can withstand moderately cold conditions, most will shut down their metabolism at about 10°C (50°F).

In general, cacti are exceptional survivors, able to endure and tolerate some of the harshest conditions, and to outlast most of their neighbours. For example, in the 1980s a population of *Copiapoa* cacti from northern Chile was able to survive an unprecedented six-year drought during which not a drop of rain fell.[2] Very intense droughts can even be advantageous to some cacti, since when most other plant life has been killed off, cacti will survive and when the rain comes again, the cacti – now free of competition – will flourish.[3]

Defining the Cactus

The cactus family is extensive and complex, comprising a vast assortment of cacti, all exhibiting unique forms and characteristics. Their definition is complicated further by a number of non-cacti that mimic the cactus – and again by some genuine cacti that do not resemble cacti at all. It is therefore useful to outline in some detail just what it is that makes a cactus a cactus.

An essential characteristic unique to cacti is that they bear small, highly specialized buds called areoles. No other plants have areoles. From these, and only from these, emerge clusters of spines. The areoles can also produce flowers, hairs (trichomes), other stems and, in some cases, leaves. Although many other types of plant have spines, they do not produce them in clusters, or from areoles.

Another unique aspect is that the spines of the cactus are in reality modified leaves. By contrast, some other plants have individual spines that grow intermittently from the surface of the plant stems; roses are an example. The more succulent varieties of the Euphorbia family, which can look almost exactly like cacti, have individual sprouting spines that are actually modified stems or shoots, rather than leaves.[4]

In the evolutionary history of plant life, cacti appear to be a comparatively late development, probably beginning to emerge as recently as 30–40 million years ago. They are most closely related to and, it is believed, derive from the family Portulacaceae.[5] All cacti originated in South America when the two American continents (North and South) were still separate land masses. As the continents merged, the cacti were disseminated first by birds, then by land

Cacti covered in snow, Arizona.

animals, into what is now North America. Birds no doubt spread the cacti to the many surrounding islands. There is one species of epi-phytic (tree-dwelling) cactus, *Rhipsalis baccifera*, which has an enormous geographic range and can be found throughout nearly all the tropical regions of the Americas. It has also become so well established on many parts of the African continent, in Sri Lanka, in southern India and in Madagascar, that many people have erroneously considered it to be native to these regions. *R. baccifera* grows among the branches of tall trees and produces sticky, berry-covered seeds that are very attractive to birds; it is believed that migratory birds from the Americas unwittingly carried some of these sticky seeds (perhaps stuck to their underfeathers) to the African continent, probably many thousands of years ago.[6]

Owing to their dramatic diversity, cacti have been classified into distinct subfamilies and tribes, and numerous genera and species. These classifications have proved somewhat fluid, particularly in recent decades. Currently, according to the 2013 edition of *The New Cactus Lexicon* (which details the findings of the International

Cactaceae Systematics Group), there are about 125 different genera encompassing some 1,500 species of cactus.[7] These numbers keep changing, particularly as new species are discovered and as existing species and genera are re-evaluated and 'lumped together' or 'split apart'. Also, because many cacti are very 'open' to hybridization through the crossing of distinct species and even distinct genera, the precise identification of some plants has historically been rather vague. More recently, DNA sequencing has revealed a great deal of new information about which plants are related to which others, and this has contributed to many reclassifications. It is conceivable that in another decade these groupings will again be radically restructured.

Currently, the cactus family is deemed to be made up of four subfamilies: Pereskioideae, Maihuenioideae, Opuntioideae and Cactoideae. The smallest of these is Maihuenioideae, which contains only two species: *Maihuenia poeppigii* and *Maihuenia patagonica*. Another small subfamily, Pereskioideae, contains about sixteen species, all belonging to the genus *Pereskia*. Surprisingly, all *Pereskia* have standard leaves. The Opuntioideae subfamily contains about twenty genera and about 300 species, nearly all of which feature glochids (tiny barbed

Copiapoa cactus, Chile.

Mammillaria cactus in bloom.

spines). This subfamily includes the well-known prickly pear cacti. The largest subfamily, Cactoideae, contains about 100 genera and about 1,200 species; it is often regarded as the most cactus-like of the subfamilies.

Most cacti are devoid of leaves, although some species of *Opuntia*, such as the prickly pear, normally produce small, rudimentary leaves on their new stem growths (these drop off as the stems mature). The South American *Maihuenia* cactus also produces some small, succulent leaves, which tend to persist even when the plant has matured. But, as we have seen, there is one genus of cactus, *Pereskia*, that produces abundant growths of traditional leaves. *Pereskia* is believed to be one of the first groups of true cactus to have evolved, and they have changed very little since. Many regard the plants as somewhat primitive, a living record of the family's early development. *Pereskia* have both traditional leaves and modified leaves (spines), and exhibit only a few of the recognizable traits of a cactus – but, importantly, they do have areoles that produce clusters of spines. It is for this reason that the emergence of spines is believed to have been the first dramatic step in the evolution of cacti.[8]

As their environment changed – and particularly as regions became increasingly arid – many of the early cacti began to adapt to the more desolate conditions. In order to survive, the plants needed to be able to endure many months or even years without rainfall. The first modification towards desert survival was the loss of leaves. Unlike leaves, spines do not lose water through evaporation. Rather, they can actually help to conserve it, providing shade and serving as a strategic insulator, surrounding the plant with a temperate layer of air to minimize the evaporation of water. They can further conserve water by helping to protect the plant from thirsty predators.

Having lost their leaves, cacti were compelled to conduct photosynthesis exclusively through their stems. Most other plants quickly develop layers of bark on their new stem growth, effectively halting all photosynthesis from occurring on those areas. To counter that, and to facilitate stem photosynthesis, cacti evolved to delay the production

Mammillaria cacti.

of bark. It is a strategy that has evolved to the point where some cactus stems can grow for 100 years or more without developing any bark, their epidermis remaining exposed and thus photosynthetically active throughout most of their lives.[9] If and when bark does develop, it is normally restricted to the lower (and thus the oldest) portions of the plant.

For photosynthesis to occur, plants must open their stomata (tiny openings in the epidermis) to let in carbon dioxide and release their waste product of oxygen. But when the stomata are open, a great deal of internal water can be lost to evaporation, particularly in very hot, dry conditions. Cacti and many other types of desert plant have developed specialized stomata that can close up and remain sealed for long periods of time – even months, if necessary. During normal conditions, they close during the day and open only at night, when it is cooler. This can save a significant amount of water. However, to cease breathing during the day can present the plant with difficulties, as it needs to absorb carbon dioxide in order to conduct photosynthesis and expel waste oxygen. Since plants cannot conduct photosynthesis in the dark – the process relies on sunlight – the strategy is to absorb

Cacti on display at Cactus Country, Australia.

Maihuenia poeppigii cactus, native to Chile, with spines and small succulent leaves.

as much carbon dioxide as possible during the night, storing it as malic acid until morning. When the sun shines again, they use this carbon dioxide 'fuel' to carry out photosynthesis once more. This process is known as crassulacean acid metabolism (CAM).[10] Since they convert the stored carbon into malic acid, cacti and other edible succulents can taste more acidic when harvested in the morning and become less so later in the day. The German scientist Benjamin Heyne first observed this 'taste difference' in 1815, but the full details of the CAM process were not defined until more than a century later.[11]

Because CAM plants pump out oxygen, and absorb large amounts of carbon dioxide at night, some have suggested that cacti make ideal houseplants, contributing to a healthier indoor environment. They can be hard at work purifying the air while the windows and doors are shut tight and other houseplants remain 'dormant'. In fact, the world-renowned environmental biologist and cactus expert Park S. Nobel has suggested that because cacti are so efficient at absorbing vast amounts of carbon dioxide quickly (in particular the prickly pear variety *Opuntia ficus-indica*), they might play an important role in future efforts to combat climate change, with the potential to serve as efficient 'carbon sinks' to capture excess carbon from the atmosphere and sequester it in their tissue.[12]

Another important evolutionary development that allowed the cactus to survive in extremely arid climates was that its stems became highly succulent. Not only did they become fatter, containing more and larger water-storing cells, but also many altered their configuration, allowing them readily to expand or contract like an accordion, depending on the availability of water. This was achieved through an innovative structure of ribs (vertical ridges) and tubercles (rounded cone-like protrusions).[13] It has been suggested that this is a more recent evolutionary development, because tubercles and, particularly, ribs do not appear in the more primitive cacti.[14]

While some non-succulent plants might comprise up to 75 per cent water, cacti can contain as much as 95 per cent water. They are also very resilient: during particularly dry periods, some can lose up to 80 per cent of their stored water supplies and still remain viable.[15] Most store their water in the form of mucilage, which has a rather slimy or gelatinous consistency. It is not known precisely why mucilage is employed, but probably it makes the storage of water more vigorous and effective. *Opuntia* and *Ariocarpus* are two groups that are known for their high concentration of mucilage, which the indigenous peoples of Mexico have used regularly to make various products, including adhesives.[16]

Most cacti are terrestrial, that is, they sprout out of the soil. Some grow to be immense, towering above the earth and stockpiling vast amounts of water in their voluminous trunks; other, smaller varieties have evolved to hide underground to avoid the sun, developing large subterranean root tubers in which to store water. Some species of *Ariocarpus* can actually pull themselves underground, leaving only the tips of their tubercles visible, during times of drought. Cacti such as these are referred to as being semigeophytic. During wetter periods they may rise up, making themselves more visible. Cultivated varieties of *Ariocarpus* normally look quite different from those growing in their natural habitat, exhibiting a much plumper,

Established prickly pear cacti, *Opuntia* sp., with woody stems.

Cacti overlooking the Uyuni salt flats, Bolivia.

This cactus, *Ariocarpus kotschoubeyanus*, grows almost entirely underground –
the triangular points on the rounded form are just visible through the dry, sandy soil.

upright form and a rich green hue. One species, *A. kotschoubeyanus*,
actually spends its entire life completely below ground; because the
crystalline, sandy soil that naturally covers it allows some light to
penetrate, these subterranean plants are able to accomplish photosynthesis. Only when they bloom do they push their flowers out
above the sand, to be pollinated.[17]

Although it is believed that cacti initially evolved to survive in very arid conditions, as their climate changed and as they spread further afield they transformed again. Some have adapted to live on some of the highest mountains, fortifying themselves against extreme cold with mounds of hair, thick, waxy skin, and densely packed spines and ribs. Many people are surprised when they first see a picture of snow-covered cacti growing in their natural habitat.

Other cacti found themselves in very moist environments, including tropical rainforests. Many of these became epiphytic, that is, they took to living in the trees – not as parasites, but using the branches as perches. This kept them away from ground-dwelling predators and brought them closer to the sun in the otherwise lush, shady forest. The Christmas cactus (*Schlumbergera* sp.) is one of the more popular of the epiphytic cacti; others are *Rhipsalis* sp., *Disocactus* sp. and *Hylocereus undatus* (which yields the popular and tasty dragon fruit). In the tropics, some cacti found their succulent nature to be an evolutionary advantage, allowing them quickly to absorb water that collected on the branches and in the crevices of trees; but most seem to have abandoned much of this capability. The stems of some species became so thin and flattened that they began to look almost exactly like normal leaves, but this was only through imitation, since they had totally lost their capacity to grow standard leaves.

Structures of the Cactus

Since most cacti do not have leaves, the shape of their stems defines their forms. Some are composed of a single stem, which can be short and globular or very tall and columnar. Others might have numerous protruding limbs. The well-known saguaro has only a single stem until it is fifty to seventy years old; only then does it begin to grow additional stems or 'arms'. *Opuntia* species (including the prickly pear) are typically composed of numerous interconnected and uniformly sized stems. As each stem reaches its maximum size, new stems grow from it, gradually increasing the mass of the plant.

The typical prickly pear cactus grows paddle-shaped segments and as a result some varieties are categorized as platyopuntia. Others in the subfamily have segments that are more tube-shaped; these are often referred to as cylindropuntia.

Many globular-shaped cacti produce offsets or 'pups' at the base of the stem. Some produce them very prolifically, forming large mounds, and these are referred to as caespitose (clump-forming) cacti. This is particularly evident in the smaller globular varieties that can be found in the genera *Lophophora, Mammillaria, Lobivia* and *Echinocereus.* It is a growth strategy that seems to be very successful on a number of levels. For example, if one or a few of the offsets are damaged, the greater clump and its remaining constituents have no problem surviving. This clumping nature can serve as an effective camouflage – emulating a pile of stones, or even a pile of animal dung (in the case of *Lophophora*). And for the more spiny varieties it can create an utterly impenetrable mass of spiky armour.

Most cactus roots remain fairly close to the ground surface and spread out extensively. This way they can quickly absorb any rain that might fall their way. The roots of an adult saguaro, for example, can radiate as far as 18 m (60 ft) from the base of the plant. Other

Epiphytic cactus. Although appearing to have leaves these are actually flattened stems.

species produce very large tuberous roots that are used to store water safely underground. These include smaller varieties such as those in the genera *Ariocarpus* or *Lophophora*, or very thin-stemmed varieties such as the night-blooming cereus (*Peniocereus greggii*), which have little water-storage capacity in the plant itself. In some species, these subterranean roots act as part of the mechanism that effectively pulls the plant underground during times of drought, for as the roots shrink from water depletion, they also pull the plant downwards. Some of the thinner fibrous roots (or rain roots) of many cacti are actually deciduous and can be shed during times of drought. Larger roots often go dormant and 'seal themselves' to minimize water loss in the soil; yet, within just a few hours of rainfall, these roots can resume water absorption fully, and they can even regrow their shed rain roots within just a few days.[18]

Cacti often reproduce by seed, but most are also adept at reproducing via stem propagation. If a stem section falls to the ground, adventitious roots (roots that emanate from the stem) form and quickly root into the soil. Most cactus growers, of course, place the stem cutting upright into the ground to encourage the roots to grow at the base, but naturally fallen stem pieces often sprout roots from whatever portion is resting on the soil. In epiphytic species, adventitious roots often form at various points on the stem even when the plant is intact and firmly entrenched. These new roots help to anchor and support the drooping weight of the plant as it spills down from the branches of tall tropical trees.[19] Some of these tree-dwelling plants are in fact hemi-epiphytic, meaning that they might also have roots that reach down into the soil, in addition to the adventitious roots that anchor themselves to the tree branches.

Wood

Many cacti possess an internal framework of wood. This is dramatically noticeable in the dead forms of the saguaro cactus, which commonly remain upright for some time after the pulp of the plant

Cacti on display at Cactus Country, Australia.

has died and rotted away. In such cases, the flexible wooden ribs sometimes splay out theatrically, no longer constrained by the tough skin and turgid pulp of the plant. The American architect Frank Lloyd Wright marvelled at the structural ingenuity of the saguaro cactus, calling it 'a perfect example of reinforced building construction . . . a truer skyscraper than our functioneers have yet built'.[20] Some cacti produce a wood that, like Swiss cheese, is full of holes (such as the cholla cactus or *Cylindropuntia* sp.), or that is divided into vertical ribs (such as the saguaro). Both structures allow a great deal of flexibility in the amount of water they can store and the manner in which it is stored. However, the timber from many established columnar cacti of Mexico and South America, such as *Trichocereus* sp. or *Stenocereus* sp., can be quite robust and fibrous, and for centuries has been used for building.

The saguaro cacti, because of their great size and protective spines, make excellent shelters for birds and small animals. Woodpeckers carve out holes in their stems; once the holes are dug out, they scar over quickly, forming a thick, woody surface – essentially a wood-lined cavern. When the cactus dies, these woody structures, along with the ribs, persist and can be found lying around on the desert floor. Sometimes, because of their shape, they can look like old, dried-out leather shoes or boots, and they are referred to colloquially as 'cactus boots'.

Spines, Glochids and Hairs

Cactus spines come in all shapes, colours and sizes. Some spines are so small that they are almost invisible; some are very pronounced, being as long as 30 cm (12 in.). Some are barbed, some thick and rather blunt, some spiralled, some straight and needle-sharp. The *Ferocactus*, which is generally barrel-shaped or takes the form of a very thick column, tends to be covered in ferocious-looking spines that are some of the longest, thickest and sharpest in the whole cactus family. Some species, in contrast, have spines that seem completely ineffectual and

Door panel made from cacti wood (*Trichocereus* sp.), Bolivia.

could not pierce their way out of a paper bag. Others have spines that are long and flat and look as though they were made of paper, such as those of *Tephrocactus articulatus*. Cactus spines come in every imaginable colour. The rainbow cactus, *Echinocereus dasyacanthus*, even has multicoloured spines on each stem, often ranged in vibrant, conspicuous horizontal bands of yellow, white, orange, pink and purple.

Spines often change size and shape as the plant matures. Most young saguaro cacti have relatively long spines (up to 10 cm/4 in.), yet when they reach adulthood their spines shorten noticeably. Similarly, many species of *Ariocarpus* have spines only when they are seedlings, and abandon them completely as adults. This strategy provides essential protection to the young plants during their most vulnerable life stage.[21] Rudolf Schulz and Attila Kapitany have cautioned against the practice of attempting to identify a cactus from its spines, which can actually be one of its most variable features, 'often differing even on

Saguaro cacti and the wood skeleton of a dead saguaro, from George Engelmann's
19th-century U.S. survey *Cataceae of the Boundary*.

the same plant as to number per areole, length, thickness and color'. There are many factors that can affect spine growth, including environment (location, soil, nutrients, light, water), the plant's age and health, as well as genetic variations – making them a most 'unstable characteristic'.[22]

Spines can help to regulate the temperature around the plant, and to provide shade from the glare of the sun. In the foggy, mountainous desert regions of the Andes, where there is very little rainfall, spines enable cacti to collect water droplets, which then run down to the base of the plant.[23] Spines can also serve the obvious purpose of protecting the plant from predators.

Glochids are the minuscule barbed spines that are produced by some varieties of cactus. These can be so small as to be invisible to the naked eye. Glochids can readily stick into the skin of a person or animal, and being so small they are difficult to remove, causing a good deal of irritation. Cactus glochids can be found on virtually all species of the Opuntioideae subfamily, including the well-known prickly pear cacti. Unlike most other cactus spines, glochids are deciduous and are normally shed after a brief growth cycle.

Hair is a very common attribute of the cactus family. Although many other plants may display faint hair growth (or pubescence) covering their leaves or stems, it is cacti that have the thickest and most conspicuous growths. These hairs (or trichomes) can serve a number of purposes. As with spines, they can regulate the temperature around the surface of the plant, both providing shade and creating an 'air buffer' that has the effect of insulating it from extreme cold and heat. Hair can also be effective in capturing water to give vital moisture to the plant. A few cacti are so completely covered that hair becomes their dominant feature: the popular old man cactus (*Cephalocereus senilis*) is totally covered in long white hair. Some, including a number of varieties of *Echinopsis* and *Trichocereus*, are generally hairless, although they often produce conspicuously hairy flower stems when in bloom.

Ferocactus sp., with bright-red-coloured spines.

Flowers

Cacti can produce some of the most striking and extraordinary floral displays of all plants. As with most outgrowths on the cactus, the flowers arise exclusively from the areoles. Cactus flowers come in just about every colour except blue, and all are produced via a unique set of pigments called betalains, a type of pigmentation that is unique

Hairy cacti.

to the cactus flower.[24] Some cacti bloom during the day, but many are nocturnal. By blooming at night and thus avoiding the daytime heat of the desert, they minimize water loss greatly. Most cactus flowers last only a short time – from just a few hours to, at most, a few days. Flowers range in size from very small (about 8 mm/ $\frac{1}{3}$ in. in diameter), as found on some *Rhipsalis* and *Mammillaria*, to very large (30 cm/12 in. or more in diameter), found on species of *Hylocereus* and *Selenicereus*.

When they reach maturity, some cacti develop a cephalium, a specialized growth of compact areoles that produce thick crops of hair, spines and, most importantly, flowers. The growth of the cephalium signals the transition to adulthood and allows the flower buds to form in a protected setting. In some genera, such as *Melocactus*, the cephalium emerges as a terminal growth (growing from the very top of the plant), which causes the base to stop growing; all effort is then directed into the development of the cephalium. Other species grow a lateral cephalium, which is often expressed as a vertical strip of hairy growth (and flowers) on just one side of a columnar cactus. In these cases both the stem of the cactus and the cephalium continue to grow.

Cacti and Animals

A variety of creatures pollinate cactus flowers: bees, butterflies, moths, bats and birds. Hummingbirds, which along with cacti are exclusively native to the Americas, are excellent and very efficient pollinators of cacti. Their ability to hover in mid-air is certainly an advantage, and, with their long beaks and exceedingly long tongues, they are adept at extracting nectar – and, as a result, accumulating large amounts of pollen, which they carry unwittingly to the next flower. There are many different species of hummingbird and each, because of its size and shape, seems best suited to pollinating a particular species. Other varieties of bird can also pollinate cacti. The curve-billed thrasher and the Bullock's oriole tend to pollinate saguaro blooms in the early morning, taking care of any flowers that the night-time pollinators

John Gould, 'Hummingbirds Feeding on Cactus Flowers', illustration from *A Monograph of the Trochilidae, or Family of Hummingbirds* (*c.* 1860).

may have missed.[25] It seems that the colours of the flowers give some indication of the type of creature that pollinates them. For example, red flowers tend to be pollinated by hummingbirds, and white ones by bats and moths.[26] Varying types of aroma also tend to attract different animals: sweetly scented flowers attract insects, while the stronger, more pungent or musky odours are more attractive to bats.[27]

Nectarivorous bats can make very effective pollinators; they can travel very great distances, have a keen sense of smell that allows them to find the aromatic flowers easily, and (like the humming-bird) are able to hover at each individual flower. Perhaps the most remarkable pollinating relationship occurs between the organ pipe cactus (*Stenocereus thurberi*) and the migratory lesser long-nosed bat (*Leptonycteris curasoae*). These bats travel enormous distances in the early spring, and their migratory route crosses forests of organ pipe cacti. Throughout the night, as they travel, they feast on the nectar of the cactus blooms, feeding and pollinating as they pass. They can cover 100 km (60 miles), drinking from as many as 100 flowers each

Melocactus azureus, a species endemic to Brazil with red-coloured cephalium.

Columnar cacti beginning to bloom.

night. Some months later the bats make the return journey along the same migratory path, this time accompanied by their young pups, feasting on the ripe fruit of the very cacti that they had previously pollinated. But on this return journey, they serve as seed dispersers, dropping the undigested cactus seeds over great distances.[28]

Generally most cactus fruit is edible, and can be readily eaten by humans and other animals. Fruits range in size from that of a pea to that of a large apple or pear. All are technically berries, and contain large numbers of small seeds among the fruit pulp; this is eaten, and the undigested seeds are then distributed across the landscape. Although some fruits have spines, hairs or glochids covering their skin, many are smooth-skinned. Since most cacti grow in fairly inhospitable environments, most have adopted a strategy that involves the production of vast quantities of seed. For example, the saguaro disperses many millions of seeds in its lifetime – but only a very few will sprout, and even fewer will make it to adulthood. Many cactus fruit burst open when ripe, making their juicy interiors (and seeds) readily available to birds and animals. Birds and bats are some of the best distributors of cactus seed, since their long-distance flights ensure a very expansive distribution.

Cacti are often the most prominent feature of a desert landscape, and with their array of spines they make excellent and well-protected homes for a range of animals. Desert rodents, especially the packrat, build their nests under the protection of the spiny cholla and prickly pear cacti, the sharp thorns of which offer protection from predators such as coyotes and bobcats. Birds find cacti to be ideal places to build their nests. Some, such as the Gila woodpecker and the gilded flicker woodpecker, dig holes in the trunks of larger cacti such as the saguaro, then nest inside. Once their eggs have hatched and the young are able to fly, they abandon these cactus caverns. Other species of bird, such as the elf owl, cactus wren and dove (those not equipped to drill holes in the cactus flesh), then move in.[29] Larger birds, including hawks and eagles, build elaborate nests high up in the arms of the saguaro. Even after the plant itself has died, the woody stems of these cacti continue to provide shelter and housing for a great number of animals, their skeletons persisting like bleached animal bones for many years in the hot, dry desert.

Gilded flicker woodpecker perched on its cactus nest.

Owl nesting in a saguaro cactus.

'Boots' made from a nest hollowed out of a saguaro cactus,
belonging to a woodpecker or an owl.

Opuntia cactus trees surrounded by seals, Galápagos Islands.

The fruit and stems of many varieties of cactus afford much-needed sustenance for a range of wildlife, including birds, reptiles and mammals. Arguably, prickly pear cacti are the most widely eaten. Numerous bird species, squirrels, coyotes and grey foxes eat the fruit, and a wide range of animals, including tortoises, gophers, jackrabbits, and even deer and the American black bear, are known to eat both the fruit and the pads. In fact, in some areas of the American Southwest prickly pear pads comprise as much as 50 per cent of the diet of the native white-tailed deer. In addition to nutrition, the cactus pads provide a valuable source of water for these animals during the summer months.[30]

two
Native Cacti, Alien Cacti
꙰

Humans have been using and cultivating cacti for many thousands of years. Because cacti are native exclusively to the Americas, historically it is the indigenous peoples of the American continents that have had the most involved and enduring relationships with them. These plants have been used for food, medicine, shelter, protection, tools and clothing – and, as a result, they have had a profound impact on human culture, religion and identity.

Pre-Columbian Cacti

There is a great deal of evidence to confirm that human societies and cacti have been closely intertwined for thousands of years. Seed deposits of prickly pear (*Opuntia* sp.) dating back nearly 12,000 years have been found in caves in the central Andes of Peru. These seeds would have been collected and used for food by the peoples living in the area. In neighbouring Brazil, ancient paintings also dating from this time have been found in the caves in the Serra da Capivara national park in Piauí. Some of these paintings appear to show opuntioid (prickly pear) cacti, specifically thought to be what is now referred to as *Tacinga inamoena*.[1] The early Peruvians, or at least their religious leaders, probably revered and consumed the columnar San Pedro cactus (*Echinopsis pachanoi*, syn. *Trichocereus pachanoi*), taking advantage of its psychoactive properties. A number of artefacts have

46

been found in the temple at Chavín de Huántar in Peru, dating back to about 1300 BC, depicting figures holding aloft large columns of this cactus.[2] There is also evidence that many of these pre-Columbian societies used cactus spines to make fish hooks, combs and other functional objects. Timber from the taller columnar cacti was – and still is – regularly used to build houses, fences, furniture and tools.[3]

The Aztec, a pre-Columbian civilization also known as the Mexica, were originally a nomadic people. They came to view the cactus in very mystical ways. In fact, cacti were central to the legend of how they ceased their wandering lifestyle and came to establish the epicentre of their kingdom, on the spot where Mexico City now stands. During the time that they existed as an assortment of nomadic tribes, the Aztecs received a very detailed prophecy that predicted the location of their 'promised land'. The prophecy stated that they would find a large lake with an island in the middle. On this island they would find a large fruit-laden cactus, and atop it would be an eagle holding a dead bird in its beak. It is claimed that in 1325 the Aztecs discovered such a sign and founded their empire on the site. In homage to this legend, the modern Mexican flag has adopted as its main emblem the image of an eagle perched atop a prickly pear

A traditional desert scene as depicted by R. Cronau, *c.* 1890.

The legend of the founding of the Aztec empire, from a 16th-century Mexican
manuscript, known as the Tovar Codex.

cactus. However, instead of a bird, as the legend claimed, that eagle
holds a snake in its beak.[4]

The Aztecs became well known for their fervent use of human
sacrifices – believing that it was only through such sacrificial rituals
that the delicate balance of the universe would be maintained. Although
most sacrifices were carried out on stone tables within temples, it

seems that in special circumstances, perhaps to impress the gods further, humans would be sacrificed on top of a large cactus. To the Aztecs, the fruit of the prickly pear had become an explicit symbol of the human heart. Therefore, the prophetic image of the eagle on the fruit-laden cactus not only marked the location of their new homeland but it foretold of the many human hearts that would be sacrificed to their gods in this new land.[5] The Aztecs also engaged in the less than lethal sacrificial act of bloodletting, in which a person would cut or pierce their own skin, usually with a cactus spine, in order to offer drops of blood to the gods.[6]

Cochineal

Another use for cacti (specifically the prickly pear, *Opuntia* sp.) in pre-Columbian times was for the production of dye. Although the dark red fruit of the prickly pear has occasionally been used as a dye, the most powerful dye substance actually comes from a small (2–4 mm/$\frac{1}{8}$ in.) parasitic insect, the cochineal (*Dactylopius coccus*), which lives exclusively on the prickly pear cactus. The male and female insects are quite different: the male has wings and can fly from plant to plant, while the female is flightless and significantly plumper. The females, which greatly outnumber the males, spend most of their adult lives with their mouths attached to the cactus pads, feeding on its juices. The insect produces within itself a strong carminic acid (carmine) that helps to protect it from predators such as ants and other insects, which find the flavour distasteful. Remarkably, this acid is coloured a deep red, and when the insect is squashed a droplet of the crimson dye emerges. When discovered by the Europeans in the sixteenth century, it was found to be far superior to any other red dye that was available either in the Old or the New World. And, depending on how the dye was mixed, it could produce hues of orange, brown, pink, red, purple or even black.[7]

Cochineal also proved to be extremely durable and long-lasting. Archaeologists have found fabrics dyed with cochineal dating back more than 2,000 years, in both Peru and Mexico. In addition to using it as a fabric dye, it was also commonly used for adornment – teeth and lips were stained with cochineal red and bodies would be painted with colourful designs. It is believed that the indigenous peoples of southern Mexico first began farming and cultivating the cochineal insect many thousands of years ago, in the Oaxaca region. The farming and cultivation of cochineal spread from there, and also became established in parts of Peru.[8]

The cultivated cochineal insect is very different from the wild versions and can in fact be regarded as a distinct species. The domesticated ones are larger and produce much more dye, which is of a richer colour. They are also easier to harvest because they do not spin thick, cottony web under which their wild cousins hide while they feed on the cactus. Without this covering, however, they are much more vulnerable to predators and inclement weather, and therefore must be diligently cared for. Extreme weather – frost or soaring temperatures, heavy and prolonged rainfall – can wipe out an entire population of domesticated cochineal. Some farmers would keep a collection of pregnant female insects and cactus pads in their homes during the winter months in order to protect them from frost. To ensure that there would be a continuous crop, during the rainy season some even transported baskets full of the insects up the mountains to higher and drier elevations.[9] When the female insects were ready to be harvested, the farmers gently swept them into a basket or bowl, then dried them in the sun for up to two weeks, before grinding them into a powder. In more recent centuries, farmers began to use ovens to hasten the drying process. It is estimated that it takes more than 150,000 dried insects to make 1 kg (just over 2 lb) of cochineal powder.

When the Aztecs conquered much of these cochineal-producing areas they in effect became administrators of the production of this dye. The native cochineal farmers were heavily taxed by their new Aztec overlords and were required to remit large amounts of the dye to the empire. The Aztec name for cochineal was *nochezli*, from *nochtle* (their name for the *Opuntia* cactus) and *extli* (blood). In 1519, when the Spanish first arrived on the continent, they were very impressed with this red dye; as they began conquering the various regions, they took over management from the Aztecs and began to exploit the production of the dye both locally and internationally. Spain began exporting cochineal dye to Europe as early as 1523, and soon had control of the world market. Later, as Portugal conquered other parts of the Americas, that country also became a major trader in the dye. Cochineal was by far superior to any other red dye that Europe – and the rest of the world – had seen before.

By the late eighteenth century, England was consuming vast amounts of the dye, principally for the fabric of its bright red military uniforms. Unhappy with the elevated prices it was charged by Spain, England yearned for its own source of the dye and attempted to set up its own production sites. Believing that Australia might be a good place to commence farming operations, in 1787 the naturalist Sir Joseph Banks ordered a large shipment of the insects to be brought to Australia. Since the Spanish and Portuguese tightly controlled the cultivated insects in Mexico and Peru, he had collected a supply of wild cochineal insects (and the cacti on which they were feeding) from Brazil. However, these proved to be a far inferior dye-producing insect to the domesticated *D. coccus*, and the insect population soon died out in Australia because the climate was too different. Eventually production was set up elsewhere, including in the Canary Islands, where it was much more successful.

For centuries this remarkable parasitic insect, the cochineal, had endured as the world's most important source of red dye. However, in the mid-nineteenth century synthetic aniline dyes, made from coal, were discovered. These proved much cheaper than cochineal, and could be produced anywhere, regardless of climate, so they soon supplanted much of the cochineal industry. These new synthetic colourants were used to dye both clothing and food. In recent years, however, as concerns about the use of these synthetic dyes in food have emerged, cochineal dye is again becoming popular as a natural

Opuntia cactus with cochineal insects, *c.* 1820, print.

Card depicting the farming of cochineal, 1907.

food colouring. It also continues to be used in limited quantities to dye fabric, colour cosmetics and other products. Cochineal has also become popular as an arts and crafts material, sold in liquid or powder form or even as whole dried insects for home use. Peru is currently the primary producer of cochineal, and in 2005 nearly 85 per cent of the world's production was carried out there; most of the remainder was in Mexico and the Canary Islands.[10]

The Pervasive Prickly Pear

No variety of cactus has spread more widely throughout the world than the genus *Opuntia* (prickly pear). While many cacti species have become endangered, both as a result of the destruction of their habitat and from over-gathering by collectors, certain varieties of *Opuntia* have actually thrived. The prickly pear has been very successful in some areas, such as the island of Sicily, where it has been grown as a fruit crop for hundreds of years, its proliferation kept in check by both natural and human means. In other places, such as South Africa and in particular Australia (with its wide-open spaces and perfect environmental conditions), the prickly pear has had a profound and

TAB. CLXXV.

EXODI Cap. XXV. v. 4.

Cochinilla.

II. Buch Mosis Cap. XXV. v. 4.

Cochenille, Scharlach.

Cochineal farming, print from the 1770s.

indeed detrimental effect. One writer bemoaned the extraordinary worldwide spread of *Opuntia*:

> Man has cut them down, and they have grown up again in greater numbers; he has grazed them with his stock, and they have spread over the prairies, mesas, foothills, and *bajadas*; he has transplanted them to new environments and transported them across the seas to new lands, and they have driven him out of his own home and taken his fields away from him, and have grown up to his very doorstep, almost closing up his home.[11]

The first *Opuntia* was probably brought from the New World to Europe some time around the 1520s, and possibly as early as the 1490s by Christopher Columbus. These plants became very popular as they seemed to embody all that was remarkable and strange about the New World. They were also extremely robust and very easy to propagate. As the maritime journeys between the Americas and Europe became more frequent, the pads and fruit of *Opuntia* were commonly carried as provisions aboard ship and eaten to fend off scurvy. It is thought that the plants were subsequently accidentally introduced wherever the ships happened to drop anchor in the course of their journeys, as a result of discarded fruit seeds and uneaten pads.[12] From Spain, the cactus was readily spread across Europe, probably to Italy by the 1570s, Germany in the 1580s and then to Holland, France and England. It is also believed that it was transported to North Africa in about 1610, when large numbers of Moorish peoples were expelled from Spain.[13]

The prickly pear was first imported to Australia in 1787 with the failed attempt to establish a cochineal industry. Although these cacti persisted, that particular variety remained well in check, and its spread was fairly limited. However, several decades later, in the 1830s, various other species of *Opuntia* began to be imported, primarily as decorative garden plants, and to serve as boundary hedges

Opuntia cacti (prickly pear) growing in Algeria, 1895.

for properties. They were initially very popular, proving to be an excellent natural fencing material, and their fruit made them even more appealing. By the 1840s many farmers were also planting large stands of these cacti as a back-up source of fodder for livestock.

In time, however, the plant began to spread widely, often by animals and also by the reckless discarding of cuttings, and it soon began to be regarded as a noxious weed. Although there were several varieties of *Opuntia* in Australia, the two main offenders were the pest pear (*O. stricta*) and, to a lesser extent, the tiger pear (*O. aurantiaca*). By the 1870s these had spread so dramatically that millions of acres in Queensland and New South Wales were rendered useless for farming or grazing. By 1900 the plant had spread over an area of 23 million ha (57 million acres). Records of a particularly badly infested area in New South Wales reveal just how quickly the cactus was spreading. Between 1908 and 1910 a 'wall' of prickly pear 'had advanced about half a mile in a solid mass on a frontage of about four miles'. In 1919 a government report describing its spread noted that

Slabs and fruit are readily detached from the plants, and may be carried for considerable distances down streams in time of flood or by cattle travelling along the stock routes. The ripe fruits are eaten by cattle and by various species of birds. The seeds pass through the intestines without injury and subsequently germinate in the droppings of the animals or birds. The birds which are the principal agents in distribution of the seeds appear to be the emu, crow, and black magpie (*Strepera graculina*).[14]

The report also mentioned that in several areas, out of desperation, there were active campaigns to destroy entire populations of these offending birds. However, it went on to caution that

No proper inquiry seems to have been made ... as to whether the harm these birds may do in this way is compensated by their value in other directions, and there is little doubt that cattle and horses are more important agents in spreading the pear than birds.[15]

Yet this caution seems to have fallen on deaf ears, as millions of emus and other birds were systematically destroyed – a practice that was encouraged by local governments who issued considerable bounties on these birds.

Numerous methods and various inventions were tried in the hope that they would help to eradicate the plant. One such invention, patented in 1912, was known as the Prickly Pear Destroyer. This machine was designed to decimate each cladode (pad or flattened stem) of the plant, so that it could not regrow. The patent for the Prickly Pear Destroyer described it as

A motor driven machine by which the pear is primarily cut by horizontal and vertically rotating knives, then carried by a shoot to a trough, where a series of stationary and

Infestation of prickly pear in Australia, c. 1915.

rotary knives further disintegrate the mass, which is then dis-
charged to the ground in front of crushing rollers, and finally
ploughed in.[16]

Unfortunately, machines such as this were effective only on very flat
farmland, not on sloping or rocky grazing land, where much of the
infestation occurred. In 1903 cochineal insects from India (*D. ceylon-
icus*) were introduced in the hope that these parasitic insects would
help to control the plant. However, they seemed to have very little
impact, and died out quickly. These insects needed to be systematically reintroduced, and at best seemed to slow the growth of only one
species of cactus, one of the least invasive forms (*O. monacantha*); they
had virtually no effect on the other species.

Although most people at this time regarded the 'prickly pear
pest' as nothing short of an invading force that required desperate
measures, there were some who took a more restrained approach.
A few even sought to proclaim its more beneficial aspects, as this
Sydney newspaper article from 1912 describes:

The prickly pear plant has frequently been referred to as one possessing many of the qualities of a good fodder plant. It is now claimed that where there is plenty of the pear plant cattle can live without water for a very long period. Hanging last week in the shop of a local butcher at Ipswich was a carcass of a cow, which is stated to have attracted a lot of attention, because of the abundance of fat with which it was covered. The animal, it is stated, lived for the six months prior to its death without a drop of water . . . If all this be true, it should be rather encouraging news to Governments and others who are trying to prevent the spread of the pear plant. There are so many uses to which this much-talked-of plant can be put, and it has so many valuable properties, so people say, that one wonders how it is there is so much of it going to waste, and why there should be so much worry about the spread of this very precious pest.[17]

But for many people, anti-prickly pear sentiment remained. Various poisons were developed and tried, and finally it was found that the highly toxic arsenic pentoxide had some effect. But this was an extremely dangerous substance, and repeated applications were required. At first it was distributed simply by being boiled in huge vats so that its vapour could waft over the fields of cacti. This method proved to be largely ineffectual, and must have been horribly toxic to the operators and anyone else in the vicinity. Later, much more targeted (and much more effective) methods, of spraying and injection, were used.

Although state and local governments were actively involved in combating the 'pest pear', in 1920 the Australian federal government formed the Commonwealth Prickly Pear Board and many additional methods were tried in order to eradicate the plant. The board's main efforts soon focused on finding a biological solution, and after much testing it found that the *Cactoblastis* moth was the best hope. This parasitic insect, which is a native of parts of South America, lays its eggs in the *Opuntia* cladodes. The larvae feed voraciously on the cactus and are capable of destroying the entire plant. After careful laboratory testing of the insects, which involved starving them of cacti to see if they would begin to eat native plants, they were imported en masse. Initially, in 1925, nearly 3,000 larvae were shipped from Argentina to Australia. They were then reared, and within a year their number had increased to 2.5 million. Following the first release, the breeding programme continued in earnest. It was found that about 25 million larvae were required to kill off a single hectare (2 ½ acres) of land heavily infested with prickly pear. It therefore proved to be an enormous undertaking, and it is estimated that in the initial four-year period some 2.7 billion eggs were released throughout the infested territories. The efforts did pay off, and as early as 1934 nearly 90 per cent of the prickly pear infestation had been destroyed – a stunning result that allowed farmers and graziers to regain much of their lost land.[18]

Cactoblastis lives on in Australia, and continues to play a role in curtailing the spread of the prickly pear. However, its long-term effect has been less dramatic. The moth has unfortunately not been effective on all species of invasive cactus, and in recent years a number of these unaffected species have begun to spread. Also, the moth does not do well in colder climates, and so there has been an invasive growth of prickly pear in cooler areas of Australia.

Yet the tale of the *Cactoblastis* moth does not end with Australia. Unlike in its native Argentina, where the moth has been naturally sequestered to a very localized area, once introduced to new regions that are free from predators and which offer a milder climate, the moth tends to flourish. After its introduction into Australia, it was taken to many other countries. Between 1933 and 1941, to combat the *Opuntia* problem in South Africa, 580 million *Cactoblastis* egg sticks were distributed, although it is agreed that its effect was not as dramatic as it had been in Australia. Later, and as recently as 1988, a very limited number of eggs were released into Kruger National Park to help control an infestation of *O. stricta*, but again with limited results.[19]

Filling a machine with arsenious trichloride.

The gas spreading over prickly pear.

Attempting to combat prickly pear in Australia using boiling vats of toxic arsenic, *c.* 1915.

In 1950 the moth was introduced to Hawaii to control its local *Opuntia* populations; it was introduced in 1957 to the Leeward Islands in the Caribbean, then to Antigua in 1962 and to Grand Cayman in 1970.[20] The moth subsequently spread to a number of nearby island countries, including Cuba, and in 1989 it had reportedly spread to Florida, and later to a number of neighbouring states of the southeastern

Living fences of cacti line the streets of old Mexico, 1892.

United States. There has been growing concern about it, particularly in the United States, since it threatens a number of native endangered cacti.

More recently, in 2006, the insect was found on a few islands just off the coast of mainland Mexico. These insects were quickly contained and eradicated, and the moth has not yet infested the Mexican mainland. Mexico is particularly worried, since it has developed huge farms of prickly pear (*O. ficus-indica*, known locally as *nopal*), and the insect is seen as a hazard to this established industry. There is also a fear that it could spread northwards into the Sonoran Desert, which spans both U.S. and Mexican territory, and destroy many native cacti there. As more and more countries begin commercial production of *O. ficus-indica*, it is feared that production would be adversely affected if even a few stray larvae were inadvertently introduced.

Cactus Fences

Cacti can make very effective barriers. Most people will hesitate before trying to climb a fence or a hedge made of cacti – even if, in actuality, it might pose little physical danger. The mere idea of coming into contact with a large cactus is often enough of a deterrent.

For centuries the tall, columnar cacti of Mexico and South America have been used to create remarkable 'living fences'. *Stenocereus thurberi* (commonly referred to as the organ pipe cactus) and several types of *Pachycereus* (or etcho) are particularly popular for making stunning and virtually impenetrable fences. In the wild, these and other related columnar cacti grow naturally close together, and even seem to flourish at close quarters. In cultivation, they are very easy to grow, and when planted in rows quickly merge into a tidy and solid barrier. It is relatively easy to create such a fence – simply cut a series of lengths from established plants and let the ends scar over for a couple of weeks, when they can be placed directly in the ground in tight rows. They will soon take root and quickly begin to grow. Such fences, some several metres high, can still be found in many parts of Mexico, and a beautiful example is prominently displayed at the Jardín Etnobotánico (Ethnobotanical Garden) in Oaxaca. In addition, the timber from these and similar columnar cacti has been used to build more traditional (non-living) wooden fences.

Perhaps one of the most infamous prickly pear fences was that planted along the border of the u.s. military base at Guantanamo Bay in Cuba. In 1962, several years after the Cuban Revolution and during escalations of the Cold War, the Cuban government planted a wide stretch of cacti as a means of preventing people from crossing to or from the increasingly contentious American base. It comprised a wall of cacti 13 km (8 miles) long and 3 m (10 ft) wide along a portion of the border of the base. In an allusion to the much-touted Soviet-era 'Iron Curtain', this barrier was quickly dubbed the 'Cactus Curtain' by the American press. *Life* magazine made special note of the 'cruel, big-needle cactuses' that now covered the area.[21] Although the cactus fence did represent a deterrent of sorts, its intended purpose may have been mainly for spectacle. The real deterrent was created when both countries planted thousands of explosive mines in the area – unquestionably a deadly deterrent. One writer has suggested that 'by drawing attention to the "cruel" cacti, the U.S. media diminished the far more dangerous minefields in the public imagination.'[22]

Although cactus fences are quite stationary, and certainly cannot go out of their way to harm us, one variety of cactus, commonly known as the jumping cholla (*Cylindropuntia bigelovii*), has garnered a very antagonistic reputation. It is so called because it appears to be able to jump out at its victims as they pass. The authors of a text on cacti published in the 1930s described the cholla in expressive and rather pointed terms:

> Cholla spines are not messengers of harmony, nor do they welcome the tenderfoot tourist in his journey across the desert, for sheathed cholla thorns constitute the most treacherous and dangerous of the cactus spines, a formidable fortress of strong, sharp, dangerously recurved spikes; and woe to the careless stranger who is inadvertently stabbed by one of these terrible cholla swords![23]

The jumping cholla has also been planted to form impenetrable barrier fences, since it is truly a plant that one would not want to climb through. Like the prickly pear and other related *Opuntias*, its primary means of reproduction results from fallen segments that take root and grow into a new plant. In the case of the cholla, the segments are so easily detached and the spines so effectively barbed that even the most careful passer-by can be pierced by one. It takes only the gentlest touch or the slightest brush against the plant and one or more of its spine-covered segments will immediately break off and readily stick into clothing, fur or skin. Because of their highly spiky nature, they can be carried a great distance by a human or animal before they finally drop off to sprout a new plant. Although we often think of cactus spines as simply protective armour for the plant, in this case they serve a far more important function – facilitating its reproductive process.

The jumping cholla's natural habitat is the deserts of the American Southwest and northern Mexico. As backpackers and mountain-bikers have travelled through these areas, there have been many unfortunate cases of a person falling off the trail into a stand of these plants and becoming covered from head to toe in spiky segments. Some victims have required urgent medical attention and hospitalization. The segments can be extremely difficult to remove, since the barbs can impale the skin quite deeply and painfully (and bloodily); each segment is covered with such an array of protruding and barbed spines that it is futile to attempt to remove the segments with one's bare hands. Tongs and a wide-toothed comb have proven to be effective tools for the removal of the segments; any remaining spines can then be pulled out by hand or with tweezers.

One cactus, commonly referred to as the horse-crippler (*Echinocactus texensis*), is a small, low-growing plant that has very strongly penetrating spines. As the common name implies, it is capable of piercing through the hoof of a horse or cow, and even through a person's shoe or boot, causing serious injury. What makes it particularly menacing is not just its spines, but the fact that its body stem is solid and does not give way when stepped on.[24] Many cows and horses have suffered injuries from this plant, much to the consternation of ranchers and cowboys.

In the early twentieth century this plant's ferocity was commandeered by the railway industry in parts of Arizona and Texas to serve as a natural, low-cost cattle guard. Cattle guards are used to prevent cattle or other grazing animals from crossing roads, railway tracks or other places where a traditional fence cannot be erected. Since the cattle quickly learned not to go near the cacti, the fences proved to be an effective guard. Below is a description from 1914 of one of the early trials of these 'cactus cattle guards':

> The first one of these guards was put in service about six months ago, and it is said that no animal has ever crossed it or shown the slightest desire to investigate it, as it consists simply of a bed of a small cactus that grows abundantly along that portion of the line and with whose thorns horses and cattle are thoroughly familiar. It is said that horses will shy

Jumping cholla cactus, *Cylindropuntia bigelovii*, native to the southwestern USA.

from a patch of this cactus as they would from a rattlesnake. This variety of cactus is said to be very long-lived, and as the material grows in abundance near by, it is not difficult to renew it if necessary. As the thorns will pierce an ordinary boot or shoe, it is necessary to place a piece of timber along the bottom bar of the fence of the guard to allow employees to cross.[25]

Cactus Graffiti

Visit any public park or botanic garden where there is an established growth of prickly pear cacti and you will probably find that someone has etched their name or other messages into the cacti's pads. It is a novel form of graffiti that appears to have traversed the globe, and can be found in places where one would never expect to find even a trace of graffiti. For example, the *Opuntia* cacti at the Botanic Gardens in Singapore – a city that is famous for being free of graffiti – were at one time completely covered in graffiti writing.

Across the world, cactus graffiti seems to be a long-standing custom, and there is evidence that people have regularly carved into

Horse-crippler cactus, *Echinocactus texensis*.

Graffiti on a prickly pear, illustration from *The Graphic* newspaper, 1883.

these cacti for well over a century. In a published illustration from 1883, a South African couple is shown standing in front of a large prickly pear growth that is visibly covered in graffiti. The man is carving into one of the pads – perhaps signing his name, or declaring his love for the woman. The caption reads: 'One way of leaving visiting cards at the Cape of Good Hope.'

This universal custom is also perhaps a reflection of the attitudes people have towards the plant. Many have regarded it as a weed, while others have considered it to be a rather curious sculpture that could be enhanced by their carving. Unfortunately for the prickly pear, 'cactus graffiti' is very easy to create. It does not require spray-paint or marker pens, and, unlike the trunk of a tree, carving into the *Opuntia* is relatively easy (a fingernail or toothpick will suffice). The etching scars over quickly and prominently, producing a thick, slightly raised line that can last for decades. As with other graffiti, examples can be found that go beyond mere lettering, including detailed renderings of human and animal figures or intricate patterns and designs.

Graffiti on prickly pear pads in Singapore's Botanic Gardens.

three

Beautiful Cacti, Beastly Cacti

🙦

I mages of cacti that date back thousands of years have been found in the mountains of Peru. A large engraved stone dating from 1300 BC, which featured a tribute to the San Pedro cactus (*Echinopsis pachanoi*, syn. *Trichocereus pachanoi*), was even found in the temple ruins of Chavín de Huántar.[1] The cactus became a common motif in the art of subsequent Peruvian cultures, as is evident in the large number of surviving pottery forms and tapestries that were produced by the Moche culture (AD 1–800). These range from decorative clay figurines to functional bowls, pots and other vessels, as well as tapestry rugs. Most often these works appear to depict either *Opuntia* (the prickly pear cactus) or the more columnar San Pedro variety. What is most intriguing about these forms is how remarkably and proficiently they could be stylized. The artists were able to capture the very essence of the cactus – its form and symmetry – yet at the same time imbue it with a distinctive stylization, something that did not happen again for many hundreds of years.

Once Europeans 'discovered' cacti they too began representing them through art and illustration. In 1535 the historian Gonzalo Fernández de Oviedo y Valdés published what are regarded to be the first printed images of cacti in his text *Historia general y natural de las Indias*. The book was based on his travels to Santo Domingo beginning in 1514. As with many early illustrators of cacti, Oviedo seemed to have difficulty depicting accurately these strange new geometrical forms; as a result, the images tended to be rather flat, condensed and simplified.[2] During the following decades, as Europeans continued to explore the globe, a number of 'travel' publications emerged that featured stylized renderings of the cactus.

By the late sixteenth century, Spanish clergy working in the Americas had begun to produce illustrated manuscripts that sought to describe how the Aztecs and other pre-Columbian civilizations lived. A typical manuscript, or codex, included illustrations depicting the interaction of these cultures with cacti: cultivating the cochineal insect on the *Opuntia* cactus, growing and eating cactus fruit, using cacti as part of religious sacrifice, and so on. Such illustrations, however, were intended more to document pre-Columbian culture than to represent cacti accurately, so the pictured cacti lack detail and are not identifiable as any particular species.

At about this time a large number of medicinal or 'herbalist' publications were being produced throughout Europe. These illustrated texts described in detail the medicinal, therapeutic and gastronomic properties of a range of plant species. One text from 1598, by the notable English doctor John Gerard, featured several illustrations of cacti. However, as with previous texts, these volumes tended not to depict the plants with any great botanical accuracy, providing instead a generalized representation while focusing on the plants' health-giving properties. Sometimes this generalization went so far as to render the depicted species almost unidentifiable. For example, in one set of illustrations from the late sixteenth century, it appears that a tall, columnar cereus has been equipped with the paddles of a prickly pear cactus. It should be noted that the Europeans were not the only ones who were depicting and publishing images of cacti; these plants found their way into the printed literature of China as early as 1688, and of Japan in 1710.[3]

By the eighteenth century more mature 'botanical' illustration had begun to emerge from Europe, providing the world with far more accurate visual representations of cacti. In 1716 the English botanist Richard Bradley produced a very important text, *Historia plantarum succulentarum* (History of Succulent Plants), one of the earliest published

Stylized bird
and cactus, Peru,
2nd century BC,
earthenware and
pigment.

texts to be dedicated solely to cacti and succulents, including several
highly detailed images of the cactus. The botanist and entomologist
William Curtis was the founding editor of *Curtis's Botanical Magazine*,
which commenced publication in London in 1787; although it covered a wide range of plants and botanical subjects, this ongoing
publication regularly featured stunning colour plates of cacti. Because
of the magazine's extensive circulation, these were some of the most
widely distributed cactus images of that era. In Continental Europe,
the apothecary Johann Wilhelm Weinmann wrote the florilegium
Phytanthoza iconographia (1737–45), which featured many images of cacti
produced by the artists Georg Dionysius Ehret and Johann Jakob

Haid. These vibrantly coloured and exceptionally detailed illustrations proved to be highly popular.

Although there were many hundreds of botanical illustrators in Europe throughout the eighteenth and nineteenth centuries, there seem to have been relatively few artists who were adept at rendering the three-dimensional forms of the cactus, or who were able to grasp the complex symmetry inherent in many of the specimens. The Swiss

Cactus print from *Curtis's Botanical Magazine*, 1838.

Epiphyllum sp., plate 14 from A. P. de Candolle, *Revue de la famille des cactées* (1829).

illustrator Jean-Christophe Heyland did appear to have an excellent understanding of the dimensional qualities of the plants, and many of his illustrations appeared in texts by the French botanist Charles Antoine Lemaire, as well as in *Mémoire sur quelques espéces de cactées* (Memoir of Cactus Species, 1834) by Augustin Pyramus de Candolle.

In nineteenth-century America, the botanist George Engelmann, whose work was featured prominently in various government

Astrophytum from Charles Antoine Lemaire, *Iconographie descriptive des cactées* (1847). Illustration by Jean-Christophe Heyland.

publications, was one of the most recognized illustrators of cacti. He was also part of the U.S. Boundary Commission, which journeyed along the border between the United States and Mexico in 1849–57 documenting the native plant life and other natural features. In 1859, as a result of these expeditions, Engelmann published *Cactaceae of the Mexican Boundary*, which featured some of the most highly regarded depictions of saguaro cacti and other native cacti of the Sonoran Desert. Later, in the early decades of the twentieth century, Nathaniel Britton (co-founder of the New York Botanical Garden) and Joseph Nelson Rose published their groundbreaking four-volume monograph on cacti, *The Cactaceae* (1919–23). This important publication became the primary source for comprehensive information on cacti for many decades. It featured hundreds of stunning illustrations, many in colour, by the English illustrator Mary Emily Eaton. Since Britton and Rose's text was the most widely studied, so too were Eaton's images of cacti.

A number of the early botanical illustrators, although striving for accuracy of detail, occasionally made significant errors in their depictions. It is possible that some of these errors were caused by the fact that the images were made from rough field sketches or shrivelled or dead plant specimens, or that essential details had been inadvertently omitted. One striking example can be found in a chromolithograph of *Melocactus* from about 1830. The image was made by Jean-Théodore Descourtilz, a botanist and renowned illustrator, and appeared in the botanical text *Flore pittoresque et medicale des Antilles* by his father, Michel-Étienne Descourtilz. The caption declares that it is a 'rouge cactus', and the entire plant is painted in a bright red hue. Although it is correct that most *Melocactus* do have a top growth (cephalium) that typically appears red, its photosynthetic base is always green. Clearly the illustrator went a bit overboard with the colour, resulting in not only a botanically inaccurate depiction, but a surprisingly surreal image.

Henry Cheever Pratt, *View from Maricopa Mountain near the Río Gila*, 1855, oil on canvas.

Some cacti, such as the giant saguaro (*Carnegiea gigantea*), were celebrated for their enormous size. In order to emphasize this grandeur in the drawn image, artists might place a human figure in the scene. This inclusion usually provided a fairly accurate sense of scale, but at other times the placement of the figure could be rather misleading, making the cactus appear to be much larger than it should be.

By the mid-nineteenth century the representation of cacti in landscape paintings had become more common. One of the most famous paintings of the Sonoran Desert, *View from Maricopa Mountain near Río Gila* (1855) by the American Henry Cheever Pratt, features a detailed rendering of a saguaro cactus set against an expansive backdrop of the desert of the American Southwest. Although the background was created from the artist's own observational drawings, the cactus forms were copied from field sketches by the botanical illustrator John Russell Bartlett. When Pratt first exhibited the painting, along with several others by him, people were amazed at how bizarre the cacti appeared. One reviewer of the show remarked:

> Some of the natural productions, introduced into these paintings, are so strange, so colossal, that nothing less than the testimony of an honorable man would entitle the assertion of their real existence to any credit.[4]

Although Pratt's depiction was more-or-less accurate, it seems no amount of naturalistic detail would have made these forms seem less alien or fabricated to the viewers of the time. Perhaps it was because he placed the unique form so prominently in an otherwise classic desert landscape that its authenticity was called into question. The structural design of the cactus is perhaps slightly contrived, but it does accurately depict the various stages of bud, flower and fruit of the saguaro, in vivid colour. It also provided a hitherto rarely seen bird's-eye view of the top of an enormously tall cactus.

The American painter Robert Julian Onderdonk took a very different approach to the depiction of cacti in his painting *Cactus in Bloom*

Postcard showcasing the enormous cactus, *c.* 1900.

Robert Julian Onderdonk, *Cactus in Bloom*, 1915, oil on canvas.

of 1915. Unlike Pratt's image, this painting strives to incorporate the cacti (*Opuntia* sp.) fully into the landscape. Although cacti are the prevailing feature of the painting, they by no means dominate the landscape. Onderdonk was closely concerned with context, and his impressionistic painting style effectively integrated light, colour and form throughout the entire image plane. Thus the cacti are not placed against a background, but are seamlessly naturalized *into* a landscape.

A number of European visual artists also depicted cacti regularly in their work. In particular, a group of German painters who were active throughout the 1920s and associated with the Neue Sachlichkeit (New Objectivity) art movement frequently featured potted cacti in their still-life compositions. These painters, including Fritz Burmann, Georg Scholz and Eberhard Viegener, tended to consider the sculptural form of the cactus plant as though it was an everyday household object – on a par with a kitchen utensil, a hammer or a lamp. Their still-life paintings in effect complicated the identity of the cactus, situating it somewhere between inanimate object and organic living form.[5]

Contemporary Artists

Numerous artists working today have incorporated images of cacti into their work. A few have been able both to capture the essence of the cactus plant and simultaneously to challenge one's perceptions of these plants.

The American painter Sharon Weiser has taken a unique approach to the depiction of the cactus. Many of her paintings feature large, heraldic groupings of many diverse species of cactus, arranged into tightly crowded scenes, an approach that often distorts the true scale of each plant. The result is a remarkable concentration of cacti, each seeming to perform as if it were a member of an urban street crowd. Although cacti are intrinsically very still forms, Weiser's seem to be full of movement, perhaps jostling and fighting to maintain their poise in the overcrowded scene. What is also striking about her paintings is the unique use of colour. Rather than limiting the palette to predictable shades of green, she imbues the cactus forms with an apparently infinite range of colour, which she applies in a manner that suggests a kaleidoscope of coloured lights illuminating the scene. Clearly she has a precise understanding of the qualities of natural light, but then appears to turn this on its head, creating remarkable scenes of diverse and vibrantly coloured cactus forms. Such fantastical renditions undoubtedly encourage us to see real-world cacti not merely as a homogeneous group of green prickly things, but as a nuanced, diverse and colourful family of plants.

The Australian artist Lucy Culliton produces paintings that emanate a strong sense of design. Her work often foregrounds simple objects, displayed in a fastidiously designed and repetitive array; since she is herself a cactus enthusiast, many of her paintings also feature collections of cacti. In her cactus paintings, Culliton seems to revel in exploring the fine line between the repetitive and the unique. For example, in *Cactus* (2004) she placed a large number of globular cacti in individual round pots and observed them from above, creating the repetition of circles as the primary design element – yet within each

Sharon Weiser, *Desert Boutique*, 2010, oil on canvas.

Lucy Culliton, *Cactus*, 2004, oil on canvas.

circle resided a unique display of detail. For a series of lithographic prints, she arranged more than forty small cacti (planted in identical square black plastic pots), but, rather than treat them in the customary shades of green, she chose the repetitive pattern of red-and-white stripes to decorate their forms. At first glance they may seem identical, but on closer observation a wide range of variations become evident. By persistently repeating forms, Culliton is able to highlight both the mundane and the extraordinary aspects of the cactus plant.

The Spanish artist Javier Mariscal created an enormous stainless steel sculpture of a prickly pear cactus, *Cactus Sculpture* (2003). It stands over 6 m (20 ft) tall, features mirrored surfaces and has numerous sections from which living *Opuntia* cacti sprout. The sculpture stands in the grounds of the Polytechnic University of Valencia, Spain.

The mirrored surfaces reflect the buildings of the sculpture's urban surroundings; smooth and sleek, they contrast effectively with the prickly nature of the cacti that both grow from it and provided the inspiration for the form. The contrast between the living cacti and the sculpture creates what has been described as 'tension between what is artificial and what is natural', as the living cacti 'fight to take over this icon which has come to substitute them'.[6]

Rearming the Spineless Opuntia (1999), an installation artwork by the American artist Amy M. Youngs, featured a small spineless *Opuntia* growing in a pot mounted on a stand. The cactus was surrounded by an armoured, motorized device that opened and closed automatically, exposing or concealing the plant. Because it was connected to an ultrasonic sensor, the plant remained exposed when no one was near it; but as soon as a viewer approached, the motor would be activated and the protective armour would snap shut. The various species of

Javier Mariscal, *Cactus Sculpture*, 2003, over 6 m (20 ft) tall, stainless steel with live *Opuntia*.

Amy M. Youngs, *Rearming the Spineless Opuntia*, 1999. Live spineless *Opuntia* cactus, motor, copper, steel, aluminium, rubber and electronic components.

Opuntia naturally have varying amounts of spines. However, owing to a long history of selective breeding (most notably by Luther Burbank around the turn of the twentieth century), the spineless *Opuntia* no longer possesses its original armour. Youngs explained: 'This sculpture embodies our nurturing impulse to protect this vulnerable, human-engineered creation.'[7] *Rearming the Spineless Opuntia* thus gives a very refreshing and empathetic assessment of cacti: rather than seeing their spines as a nuisance or even a threat to humans, Youngs reminds us that they are intended to be purely defensive appendages by which to protect the plants from aggressors. They are not offensive weapons. She manages to address these ideas in a very playful manner, but it represents a perspective that is often overlooked when considering the cactus.

Prickly Words

In his satirical comedy *Dreaming of Babylon* (1977), the quirky counter-culture writer Richard Brautigan used the characteristic qualities of the cactus to amplify the dangers of a heavy fog. In one passage, he described a thick fog that had descended on the town, one that – like many heavy fogs – was much too dangerous to drive in. But this particular fog had an even more dangerous quality, and he referred to it as 'a cactus fog . . . it was the worst kind of fog because it had sharp spines on it. It made moving around in it a very dangerous proposition. It was best to stay where you were at and just wait until it went away.'[8] We are all familiar with the sensible advice that one should avoid driving in heavy fog so as not to risk an accident, but it is never the fog per se that is the danger, rather the lack of visibility it causes. In this story, Brautigan humorously depicted the fog as having an intrinsically menacing nature. It seems everything, even a fog, can be transformed into an aggressor with the addition of a few cactus spines.

The folklorist, writer and 'urban legend' expert Jan Harold Brunvand has recounted the enduring fictional story that tells how a woman brought home a recently purchased cactus plant and displayed it proudly on her coffee table. Although it was covered in spines, she thought it the perfect addition to her home, and she would often linger near it, admiring its strange beauty. However, one day the cactus suddenly began to tremble and move about from its own impetus. Horrified, the woman rang the authorities. When she described the increasingly violent nature of the quivering cactus, she was told emphatically to 'get away from it and to leave the house immediately'. However, before she was able to do so the cactus violently exploded and, along with the spines, thousands of newly hatched poisonous spiders shot out across the room. It was then revealed that several tarantulas had laid their eggs in the plant, and all had hatched at precisely the same moment, causing the plant to explode.[9] This legend is essentially an amplified 'Trojan horse' narrative, in which the cactus (already a threatening form) becomes the transporter of an even greater threat.

There are also various superstitions, traditional tales and religious beliefs that involve the cactus. According to the botanist Roy Vickery in his *Dictionary of Plant-lore*, in Hungary and several other European countries cacti are traditionally considered to bring bad luck. Cacti can also be considered in positive terms, for example, according to English folklore, watering your cactus on Christmas morning is said to bring good luck.[10] In Brazil, some believe that if you throw a *Melocactus* onto the roof of your house and it takes root, you will have good luck – and that the plant will also help to keep away such evils as witches and violent storms.[11] In La Aduana, in Sonora, northwestern Mexico, there resides what is perhaps the most highly revered cactus in the world. This 'holy cactus' grows out from the vertical stone wall of a historic Catholic church. The plant is nearly 3 m (10 ft) tall and is believed to be more than 250 years old. Legend has it that it first sprouted from the stone wall some time in the 1730s and soon afterwards a vision of the Virgin Mary appeared standing among the cactus stems. Because of this story, thousands of pilgrims (and tourists) visit the cactus each year.[12]

The disparaging attitude that is so widespread towards cactus plants has fuelled the emergence of a number of interesting linguistic phrases. For example, one might say that something 'is cactus', which suggests that it is dead or finished, or at least in a very hopeless situation that cannot be overcome. Another phrase, to be 'out in the cactus', suggests that one is in the middle of nowhere, far removed from civilization.[13]

Cowboy Cacti

Cacti have become an important part of the iconography of American Wild West mythology. Any book or film that deals with the genre of the western invariably features cacti as part of its *mise en scène*. In these narratives, cacti not only help to establish a specific location

A most unlikely scenario for obtaining fresh water, as water does not flow from cacti, c. 1900.

– the American Southwest – but exemplify the pervasive hardships and dangers that the protagonists of these stories must endure. The classic western author Zane Grey described in *The Rainbow Trail* (1915) how the main character had become hardened by his many years in the desert: 'The desert had transformed Shefford. The elements had entered into his muscle and bone, into the very fiber of his heart. Sun, wind, sand, cold, storm, space, stone, the poison cactus, the racking toil, the terrible loneliness.'[14] Notably, Grey lists 'poison cactus' as one of the hardships. It seems cowboys were always being confronted with poisonous foes – from poisonous rattlesnakes and poisonous scorpions to 'Indians' shooting poison-tipped arrows. Thus, by having their spiky nature conflated with these venomous dangers, the plants erroneously became not only an obstacle to avoid but a most deadly adversary. In another novel by Grey, *Nevada* (1928), one exceptionally dangerous gunman, Cedar Hatt, is described as being 'cactus an' side-winder rattlesnake mixed up with hell'.[15]

But, on occasion in these stories, the cactus represented salvation for these desert protagonists. Many stories have told of how a dehydrated traveller, near death with thirst, is saved by a water-filled cactus. In a last dying effort he takes his knife, slices into the flesh of the cactus and drinks the cool, refreshing water inside. Unfortunately, such tales are quite impossible, since cacti do not store their fluid reserves in this way. Although many are 90 to 95 per cent water, it tends to be stored as rather slimy mucilage, and is never available as a free-flowing fluid – let alone pure or palatable water. Some cacti, such as the prickly pear and a number of barrel cacti, are quite edible and provide some degree of hydration if eaten. However, a cowboy would be much better off in these stories if he encountered a stand of cacti laden with ripe fruit, since that would definitely provide refreshment.

Cactus Flowers

In *Plant Lore, Legends and Lyrics* (1892), Richard Folkard paints a some-what disparaging picture of cacti, describing them as having 'weird and grotesque columns or stems [that are] devoid of leaves'. Rather than being plant-like, he describes them as more akin to 'imperish-able statues'. Folkard does make one concession, however – as many do – admitting that 'the splendid colours of the cactus flowers are in vivid contrast with the ugly and ungainly stems.'[16] Regardless of what people may think about cacti, nearly everybody can appreciate their vivid floral displays. It is something that seems constantly to surprise, and even a veteran cactus enthusiast still marvels when their plant suddenly 'comes to life' in a brilliant floral display.

Perhaps some of the most remarkable cactus flowers belong to the night-blooming queen of the night, *Selenicereus grandiflorus*. As do many cacti, this thin-stemmed climbing plant produces flowers that seem to be far beyond its capability. The blooms, which are a brilliant white and grow up to 30 cm (12 in.) long, have had perhaps the most enduring impact of all cactus flowers on public opinion, and have been highly romanticized. A famous early depiction can be found in Robert John Thornton's book *The Temple of Flora* (1807), in a remark-able image painted by Philip Reinagle, with background by the landscape painter Abraham Pether. It features the large flower very prominently in the foreground; in fact, the bloom nearly fills the entire frame, and just a portion of the thin stem of the cactus is visible, clinging to the trunk of a tree. In the background the full moon illuminates the scene, and the face of a large clock tower declares the significantly late hour: two minutes past midnight. These remarkable flowers, which open only at night, seem to epitomize the traditional romance of warm summer nights and moonlit strolls. Their enveloping fragrance and bright white display seem not only to dominate the night, but to dominate and transform one's thoughts about cacti.

In fact, a wide range of night-blooming cacti have gone by the name 'queen of the night'. One is the night-blooming cereus, *Peniocereus greggii*, a native of the southwestern United States, particularly Arizona. Its flower is especially celebrated because it blooms for a single night just once a year, and sometimes only once every two or three years. In more tropical regions of the United States, particularly Hawaii, the epiphytic cactus *Hylocereus undatus* (producer of dragon fruit) has also been referred to as queen of the night. In the early and mid-twentieth century these flowers were frequently used to promote the island's tourism industry. Because Hawaii is often marketed as a destination for couples, in particular newlyweds, the romance of these blooms was deftly exploited. Not surprisingly, it was at about this time that night-blooming cacti began to be incorporated as a recurring thematic element in a number of mainstream romance novels. And, to cement their place in our romantic psyche, many different perfumes have been produced that purport to capture the essence of these night-blooming flowers. In the late 1940s the perfumer Howard K. Foncanon launched his original cactus-flower perfumes as part of his 'Perfumes of the Desert' series, his most popular scent being Midnight Cereus. These were at first sold exclusively from his shop in Albuquerque, New Mexico, but later they achieved wider distribution.[17] Since then many of the largest perfume brands have followed with their own versions, including Christian Dior, Prada and Aedes de Venustas.

Philip Reinagle (flower) and Abraham Pether (background), 'The Night Blooming Cereus', published in Robert John Thornton's *The Temple of Flora* (1807).

Sitting on a Cactus

Some people continue to be irrationally terrified of cactus spines – an actual neurosis that has been termed 'kaktosophobia' – even though many other types of plant are capable of causing much greater harm. For example, the thorns on a rose or blackberry bush can be very painful, poison ivy can become an extreme irritant, and merely touching the sap of some species of *Euphorbia* can cause tremendous pain, swelling and illness. Yet there is something about the physical nature of cacti that worries many people, and we seem to be particularly worried about *sitting on* a cactus plant and consequently getting pricked by its spines.

Many are taught from a very early age to be wary of this. For example, a well-known children's book, *Hop on Pop*, by the author and illustrator Dr Seuss features a character called Pat. Pat seemed to have a penchant for sitting on odd things; he sits on a baseball bat and then on a cat and nobody seems to mind too much. But then, just as he is about to sit on a cactus (a large prickly pear), another character yells in utter panic: 'NO PAT NO Don't sit on that.'[18] As a result of this insistent warning, Pat just misses sitting on the cactus. From the perspective of the child reader, he narrowly avoids a calamitous injury.

The misfortune of sitting on a cactus has also been the subject of countless postcards, cartoons and humorous illustrations. One typical humorous travel postcard from the American Southwest from the 1890s depicted a man being pricked on the rear end by a spiky cactus; the caption read, 'I'm stuck on the country here!'

A popular travel postcard from the American Southwest, *c.* 1930s.

'Prickly Pair', a cactus-themed chair set designed by Valentina Gonzalez Wohlers and constructed in a variety of designs and patterns.

In 1953 this rather pervasive form of kaktosophobia was humorously subverted by the Naugatuck Chemical Company (a division of the United States Rubber Company) in order to market their innovative furniture cushioning materials. The company manufactured a latex compound that was mixed with 'springy cactus fibers' to form the stuffing material for their cushions (the cacti used were probably either *Cephalocereus* or *Pilosocereus*).[19] The advertising campaign featured an image of a sophisticated woman sitting comfortably on a sofa in a cactus-filled desert, accompanied by the text: 'Ever sit on cactus? Believe it or not . . . that's exactly what this lady's doing . . . relaxing on a cushion of cactus!'

Interestingly, one designer has managed to turn the cactus form into a particularly stylish chair. The Mexican furniture designer Valentina Gonzalez Wohlers produces large beautifully designed prickly pear-inspired chairs that ironically play on the idea of 'sitting

Vintage and contemporary cactus kitsch.

Ceramic cactus lamp.

on a cactus'. The chairs are produced in a variety of styles and patterns, with some having faux cactus spines protruding from the cushioned parts (actually soft, harmless fibres), adding to the cactus aesthetic. In a linguistic play on the word 'pear', Wohlers refers to the set of two chairs as a 'prickly pair'. The chairs, which are produced in both Mexico City and London, convey a very streamlined design but, because they feature the highly iconic and immediately recognizable interlocking oval-shaped stems, they are readily interpreted as the pads of the prickly pear cactus.

Cactus Things

A plethora of cactus-themed objects has been produced over the last century or more, whether inexpensive tourist trinkets and every-day household objects or expensive designer pieces. Depictions have ranged from the relatively abstract to the exceedingly realistic. Perhaps the earliest and most common mass-produced cactus-themed objects appeared in the late nineteenth century, predominantly taking the form of traditional dinnerware that featured detailed images of cactus flowers, particularly the large night-blooming cereus. By the early twentieth century, there began to appear a much wider range of both decorative and utilitarian cactus-themed objects. The kitchen, in par-ticular, seemed to become an epicentre of such items. Thus countless versions of cactus-decorated silverware, tea towels and oven gloves, and cactus-shaped salt and pepper shakers, candles, biscuit cutters, cake tins, cookie jars, teapots, cups and bowls have become commonplace.

Over the decades, as more items have been produced, and as more people have become acquainted with the cactus, their depiction has become increasingly sophisticated. The most intriguing images tend to be those that playfully subvert the expected characteristics of the cactus. For example, there are many objects that encourage the user to 'interact' with depictions of cactus spines in rather surpris-ing ways. A popular cactus-shaped pen, for instance, requires the user to hold the 'spiky' part of the cactus (which is in reality soft and

Cactus-themed pens (large) and erasers (small).

squishy) in order to write. One boldly styled saguaro-shaped ceramic lamp, contextualized in a white flower-pot motif, uses light to form its 'spines'; the entire surface of the cactiform lamp is covered with small pinholes that allow the interior light to shine through. When the lamp is turned on, the light shines out of these holes, creating illuminated 'spines' of protruding light beams. Various cactus-shaped novelty toothpick-holders and pincushions have also been marketed. In order to serve their function, the user must first stick an array of toothpicks into the toothpick-holder or pins into the cactus-shaped pincushion. Inserting the 'spines' both makes it a functional object and completes the representation of the cactus.

Cactus-print toilet paper.

At least one manufacturer has produced cactus-themed novelty toilet paper, which features colourful images of cacti printed on each individual sheet. Such imagery, of course, plays on the fear of (or at least aversion to) having cactus spines pricking one's bottom. Since most toilet-paper manufacturers seek to promote their product as being exceedingly soft and luxurious, it is rather unexpected to have one that ostensibly subverts this idea.

four

Almost Human:
The Anthropomorphic Cactus

W e are all familiar with cartoon-like images of cacti – often adorned with expressive faces and 'arms' held high. Since the nineteenth century, representations of cacti have regularly been imbued with distinctly human characteristics, in everything from paintings and sculpture to comics and animation.

Humans are naturally inclined to anthropomorphize, or imbue things with human characteristics, particularly in the visual arts. There has been an innumerable array of objects and animals that have been personified in this way, whether as the distinctly human-like dog Snoopy, in the comic strip *Peanuts*, or the animated bird known as Donald Duck, or the human-faced train of Thomas the Tank Engine. According to the theorist and professor of animation Paul Wells, we live in a world of objects and creatures that are very different from ourselves, but we are able to make them somewhat more accessible through the visual arts 'by the imposition of human character traits that render material and natural artefacts familiar'.[1] The visual anthropomorphism of other living things (plants and animals) provides a unique opportunity to creatively bridge our biological differences – helping us to understand the traits we share with other life forms.

Plants in general, and cacti in particular, occupy an interesting space in our world: we know they are alive, yet they do not visibly display 'life' in the same way that humans and animals do. Intellectually, we know that plants are internally 'alive', yet outwardly they can look completely inert. Apart from a few exceptions, such as the Venus flytrap, their movement is virtually invisible to us. In fact, many cacti look more like carved sculptures than anything that might be alive, let alone growing and moving. Yet when we revisit a plant after a few weeks, we can marvel that it is slightly taller, that it has a new growth or a new flower. Movement and growth have unquestionably occurred, we have just not been able to witness them as they have happened. We understand that there is more going on within the plant than we can see.

Scientific investigations into plant life became robust in the mid- to late nineteenth century, and it was at about this time that scientists began discovering the remarkable 'hidden' behaviour of plants. Much was learned about how plants functioned – how they 'breathed', reproduced, consumed and manufactured nutrients and, perhaps most intriguingly, how they grew and moved. It is no surprise that, during this era of remarkable discovery into the complexity of plant life, a number of artists (particularly in France and Germany) began to anthropomorphize plants, including cacti. These unique depictions could be seen as a way of articulating the extraordinary life that resides within these plants, just beyond our perception.

Ceramic cacti figurines.

Hairy cacti adorned with hats and glasses, on display at Cactus Country, Australia.

The Human Nature of Cacti

Cacti possess many physical features that can remind us of ourselves. One remarkable characteristic is that many varieties of cactus have hair – in some cases rather long, human-like hair. In common with humans and other mammals, cacti generally grow hair for protection: shade from the sun, and warmth in freezing temperatures. The great abundance of hair on some species has been acknowledged in their common names, such as *Cephalocereus senilis*, the old man cactus. When you touch the hair of a particularly bushy specimen, it is remarkable how mammalian it can feel. As the plant gets older, it may lose some of its lower hair, and the fresher growth near the top can accentuate the look of human hair on top of its head.

In humorous illustrations, this particular trait has been exaggerated to suggest a human-like character. One particular cartoon illustration from about 1890 portrays a group of exceptionally hairy cacti on display at the Royal Botanic Gardens at Kew, west London. Although in the drawing the cacti appear to have slight facial expressions and subtly defined limbs, it is their prominent heads of hair that emphasize their humanistic affinity. The text within the illustration reads: 'Visitors are requested not to touch the plants.' However, the families that are viewing them appear to be more concerned that the long-haired creatures might reach out and touch *them*.

Some cacti, including a number of varieties of *Trichocereus* (syn. *Echinopsis*), are generally hair-free except when they flower. As the plant develops flower buds, the buds often grow a very thick, coarse, dark crop of hair, particularly along their maturing flower tubes. These prominent hair growths that surround the plant's reproductive

Illustration from a magic lantern glass slide, *c.* 1900.

organs have a striking resemblance to pubic hair – which is, in fact, an almost unique human trait: most scientists agree that it is not generally found in the rest of the animal kingdom.[2] For both humans and cacti, this hair is a means of protecting their sensitive areas. Cactus flowers are much more prone to sun damage, water loss, predators and stark changes in temperature than the rest of the plant, which is more resilient. Scientists have also suggested that humans developed pubic hair to serve as a sort of primitive reservoir for the absorption and wafting of human pheromones.[3] Several species of *Trichocereus*, which have some of the hairiest flowers, are generally night-blooming cacti and rely heavily on the strong aroma of their flowers to attract bats and other olfactive pollinators. Although the notion is speculative, it is plausible that having odour-trapping hair surrounding the flower might be of some benefit in helping to waft the floral aromas into the air.

One mutated form of cactus, *Mammillaria elongata* 'Cristata', is commonly referred to as the brain cactus because of its crested (mutated) growth that appears to mimic the gnarled form of the human brain.

Hairy cactus flower.

'Brain' cactus, *Mammillaria elongata* 'Cristata', in a novelty planter.

These plants are often sold in novelty pots in the shape of a human head or skull. Another brain-like form, *Stenocactus multicostatus*, is also referred to as the brain cactus – although this species' brain-like formation represents its normal growth and is not a mutation. Other cacti with 'human' traits and common names are the bishop's cap (*Astrophytum myriostigma*), a very slow-growing, spineless cactus that can reach a height of 40 cm (16 in.) or more, its shape and generally whitish-grey colour giving it a resemblance to a bishop's hat, and the monk's hood cactus (*Astrophytum ornatum*) and the 'old lady' cactus (*Mammillaria hahniana*). The *Melocactus*, on maturity, produces a unique bright red cephalium (the word derives from the Latin for head) composed of compacted wool, bristles and flowers. For this flower-producing growth, which rests incongruously on top of the normal green photosynthetic base, the plant has been referred to as the Turk's cap cactus, since the red cephalium resembles the traditional Turkish fez.

The Saguaro Cactus

No species of cactus has been personified as widely as the saguaro (*Carnegiea gigantea*). The saguaro, which grows to enormous height – 15 m (50 ft) or more – is an imposing form in the barrenness of the desert, and can readily be interpreted as having human-like characteristics. It is said that when, in the mid-sixteenth century, Spanish explorers first encountered forests of saguaro in the Sonoran Desert of Arizona, California and northwestern Mexico, they dubbed it 'the land of the marching giants'.[4] More recently, the artist and cartoonist Reg Manning (of whom more later) remarked in his enduring book on cacti (first published in 1941):

> Driving through a Saguaro forest for the first time makes you a little self-conscious. You get the odd feeling of walking into a crowded room, where everybody stops what he was doing and watches in embarrassed silence till you have passed through. The larger ones, with their dozens of twisted arms, seem to have been 'frozen' in the midst of some wild dance-orgy. Others huddle together as though they had been caught chortling over a particularly juicy bit of local scandal.[5]

It would seem natural for anyone seeing these cacti to perceive the relatively simple form as a body with raised arms. Over the years countless collections of photographs have been published that attempt to capture saguaros that exemplify this.

A number of cultures have traditionally taken an animistic view of the world, in which they consider that most natural forms possess souls, or at least a certain kind of 'liveliness'. Historically, many groups of Native Americans have viewed the world in this way, so it is not surprising that their perception of the saguaro has been coloured accordingly. The Tohono O'odham ('Desert People') consider the saguaro to be not just cactus, but very much alive – essentially the same as humans. In fact, their legend describes how the first saguaro actually originated as a human girl.

The legend explains that one day a mother said goodbye to her young daughter (Sugu-ik Oof) and set out for the nearby village to look for food. Not wanting to be left behind, the girl followed her mother, but she soon became lost and resorted to asking various animals if they could help her to find the village. But the animals were selfish and would not help her. Finally, a little grey bird offered to show her the way, but by the time she reached the village, her mother had already left. She then asked some of the local children for help, but they simply mocked her. As they continued to taunt her, much to their astonishment she began to sink into the ground. The horrified children went to find the girl's mother, but by the time they returned with her the girl had vanished completely into the earth. Her mother was, of course, devastated, and laid out food and water for her at the spot where she had disappeared. Soon a large cactus began to grow there; it flourished, and quickly grew to a great height. It bloomed, producing beautiful white flowers and then bright red fruit. The grey birds that had been kind to the girl came and ate nearly all the fruit. This made the children of the village angry, so they began to throw rocks and spears at the birds to chase them away. In response, the cactus suddenly disappeared. The mother and villagers found it some days later on a nearby hillside. They asked the cactus why it had gone away, and the girl-cactus replied that she had been repaying the birds for their kindness: if the children would not let the birds eat her fruit, then no one could. As a result, the people, the birds and the animals all decided that from then on they would no longer fight over the fruit, but would share it equally.[6]

Another group of people, the Seris, who are native to the Sonoran Desert on the west coast of Mexico, have traditionally identified and connected with cacti in a unique manner. In the area where they live grow very large columnar cacti that are commonly known as sahueso (*Pachycereus pringlei*). When a child is born, the parents choose one of these cacti, and bury the placenta at the base. For the rest of the

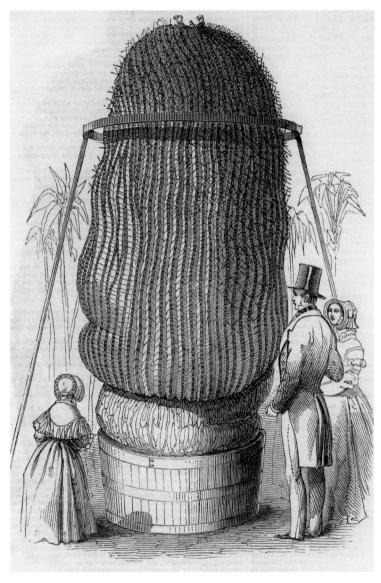

'Monster Cactus' at Kew Gardens, 1846.

child's life, and even after their death, that cactus is linked closely with them – in a sense, it is a living embodiment of that person.[7]

Convalescent Cacti

By the mid-nineteenth century there were significant collections of cacti in many of the major botanic gardens outside the Americas. One of the most celebrated was that of the Royal Botanic Gardens at Kew, which became well known for importing remarkable specimens. The acquisition of a particularly large example would often be regarded as a newsworthy event, and articles and images were published in the newspapers. Unfortunately, some of these larger specimens did not long survive the voyage from the Americas, being diseased and sometimes rotten by the time they arrived. In 1846 the *Illustrated London News* reported that a particularly large 'Monster Cactus' had arrived recently from Mexico. The cactus measured 3 m (10 ft) in circumference, was almost the same in height and weighed more than a ton. The paper published an extraordinary illustration of it, but conceded that the public would not in fact be able to see the 'Monster' in the flesh, for it had become sick and was dying.

'Convalescent cactus being taken out for an airing in Kew Gardens', *Punch*, 1931,
© Punch Ltd.

On its arrival, it appeared in the most perfect condition, and threw out flowers in a few weeks, from the crown, or top of the plant; but, in the present instance, these efforts, like the reputed song of the swan, were only indicative of its dying state.[8]

However, the article continued, 'The Garden still boasts of the former, or original "Monster Cactus" in high health and vigour.' Other articles of the time mentioned ailing cacti and the remarkable efforts undertaken by the staff of Kew to save them. After a while members of the public must have become enamoured of these strange 'creatures' that would take ill and then die, or after great effort be brought back to 'good health'. It must also have seemed strange to some readers that a 'sick' cactus would be the subject of such a high-profile news story – rather than, more appropriately, a convalescing aristocrat. In 1931 *Punch* magazine published a cartoon that effectively gave voice to this perception. The cartoon depicts a visibly ill, human-sized anthropomorphic cactus sitting in a wheelchair pushed by an attendant in a park-like setting, accompanied by a very professional-looking nurse. The caption reads: 'Convalescent cactus being taken out for an airing in Kew Gardens.'[9]

Artists and Illustrators

In countries such as France and Germany, cacti were fairly common by the mid-nineteenth century. Although still regarded as exotic, they were increasingly prevalent, and many homes had a plant or two – perhaps perched prominently on a sunny windowsill. A number of nurseries featured large selections of cacti, although, other than those at Kew Gardens (and a few other botanic gardens), most available cacti would have been relatively small, allowing them to live indoors during the cold European winters. It therefore made

Opposite: Carl Spitzweg, *The Cactus Enthusiast*, 1850, oil on canvas.

sense that cacti were generally depicted in the visual arts as small potted plants.

Carl Spitzweg was a German realist painter who created a number of paintings that featured cacti. One of his more famous images is *The Cactus Enthusiast* (1850), in which a man stands in front of an open window, looking curiously at a small cactus that sits on the windowsill. The man and cactus look oddly similar; both are captured in a dynamic pose with their 'heads' tilted to one side as they seemingly gaze fondly at each other. The man wears a long cactus-green overcoat, his bald head strikingly similar to that of the cactus. The painting appears to capture a very brief moment – and to emphasize this fleeting moment, the artist incorporated a large clock on the wall. The pendulum is poised in an extreme leftwards swing, as if captured by a high-speed camera. It is as though Spitzweg has caught the precise moment at which not only the pendulum has swung far to the left, but both the man and the cactus have cocked their heads in reciprocal gazes. We expect that in the next moment the pendulum will swing to the opposite side and both man and cactus will right themselves. Although the portrayal of this particular cactus expresses only limited notions of anthropomorphism, its context and its relationship with other elements in the painting make it decidedly human-like.

In France, in the mid-nineteenth century, a growing trend in art and illustration seemed to encourage the anthropomorphism of just about everything from the natural world, from flowers to zebras. The artist Odilon Redon, painting in this tradition, created many images that conflated humans with other living creatures. He was also greatly influenced by Darwin's theories of evolution and the growing mainstream interest in natural science that was sweeping the country.[10] In 1881 he made *Cactus Man*, a charcoal drawing that combined the head of a man and the spines of a cactus, all neatly planted in a ceramic pot. Intriguingly, Redon, who wholeheartedly rejected realism in his work, did not portray these spines as being outwardly threatening. Instead, he inverted the entire concept of cactus spines, depicting the Cactus

Odilon Redon, *Cactus Man*, 1881, charcoal on paper.

German postcard, *c*. 1900.

Man wearing them (as some have described) as a 'Christ-like' crown of thorns, as if they were stabbing into him and were the cause of his own pain and suffering.[11]

A number of nineteenth-century German illustrators regularly anthropomorphized the cactus plant, usually as a small, rather cute creature – generally quite harmless, albeit somewhat exotic and eccentric. The Lilliputian scale of many of the cacti depicted in this way, of course, reflected the size of the specimens with which most people would be familiar in their everyday lives. One exceptionally popular series of postcards from the 1890s featured many different species of anthropomorphized cactus. The diminutive size of the cacti is emphasized by the inclusion of butterflies and beetles, which by comparison seem to be the size of dogs or large birds. Each postcard in the series featured two or three cacti interacting. On one card, two elderly female cacti (*Echinocereus* and *Echinocactus*) are busily knitting and gossiping together. In another, a female *Opuntia*

Diego Rivera, *Landscape with Cacti*, 1931, oil on canvas.

and a male *Astrophytum* seem to be quarrelling. In a third, a female *Echinocereus* and a male *Echinocereus* of another species, both in full bloom, seem to be engaged in a fiery courtship.

In Mexico, the painter Diego Rivera, famous for his politically themed murals, painted many images of the flora and fauna of Mexico, and many included cacti. In contrast to most European illustrators, who were inspired by the meticulous collecting of small and exotic specimens, Rivera took as his subject the large, native cacti of the Sonoran Desert and surrounding areas. Cacti, in effect, constituted and helped to define his native land. Several of his paintings feature decidedly anthropomorphic cacti. *Landscape with Cacti* (1931), for example, depicts a group of saguaro cacti — one of them clearly female, with not only cactus 'arms' but cactus 'breasts'. In *Cactus on the Plains* (1931), Rivera depicts what is probably a loose representation of two organ pipe cacti, intended to be read as a pair of giant hands rising from the desert floor in a dramatic grasping motion.

North of the border, in the United States, there lived another artist who was greatly influenced by the monumental cacti of the surrounding Sonoran Desert. The well-known illustrator and cartoonist Reg Manning created a steady stream of political cartoons, books and illustrations, and was known best for his personified cactus illustrations and cartoons, which he began to publish in the 1930s. His book *What Kinda Cactus Izzat?* (1941) became very popular and has been reprinted many times. His cacti are always depicted as friendly creatures, full of vigour, although they can be rather cheeky sometimes, as they seem to delight in pricking unsuspecting tourists' rear ends. Manning undoubtedly played an important role in popularizing the anthropomorphic cactus image, particularly that of the Saguaro, in American popular culture. His work clearly had an influence on the animators who worked for Walt Disney, and on the work of the renowned American cartoonist Charles M. Schulz.

Peanuts

The comic strip *Peanuts* (1950–2000), created and drawn by Schulz, features the familiar anthropomorphized dog Snoopy. Snoopy has a cousin named Spike, a very thin creature who lives a lonely, hermit-like existence in the desert and, having no one else around, talks to and interacts with the local cacti. These comic strips take a subtle approach to the anthropomorphism of these cacti, since they do not depict any overtly human characteristics (except for the natural 'arms' of the saguaro), and the plants do not 'speak'. Yet Spike is able to 'speak' to and interact with them, and he seems to believe that they respond, by moving and speaking back to him. We, the reader, never see any direct indication of these actions, nor read any speech balloons coming from the cacti; the actions only occur between the panels of the comic strip, and ultimately only within Spike's imagination.

In one example, Spike informs a nearby saguaro cactus that he will be 'going into town for a while', and reassures him: 'Don't worry, I'll be back before dark.' The cactus, of course, remains motionless, with its arms held up, one slightly higher than the other. As Spike walks away, he remarks: 'It's nice to have someone miss you when you're gone.' In the final panel, he turns to look at the now distant cactus and says: 'When I look back I can see him still waving.' Of course, in this example the reader never sees any evidence that the cactus has moved; in fact, it is drawn in exactly the same pose and from the same angle in every panel. But it is the imagination of Spike, articulated through his thought balloons, that allows the reader to understand the events from his perspective.

In another example, Spike can be seen 'square dancing' with a group of cacti. The cacti of course remain stationary, and it is Spike who does all the dancing and racing around from one cactus to another. But each time Spike 'holds hands' with the cacti during the dance, the spines stab him painfully. In the end he can be seen seated on the ground, his hands heavily bandaged and throbbing with pain. It is, in fact, a self-induced injury that is the result of an imagined dance with some very stationary cacti that just happen to be posed a little like dancers in mid-step.

In all the strips that feature Spike and his cactus friends, we see only sequential still images, yet we are allowed to imagine that the cacti have been moving between the panels just as Spike has been imagining. Because the movement of the cactus resides within Spike's imagination, it is also available to us, the readers, in our imagination as we fill in (perhaps 'mentally animate') the action that occurs between the panels. This is one of the reasons why these strips are so effective and resonate so well with their readership. We, the readers, are familiar with the long-standing tradition of imbuing cacti with human personas and actions, and although we know that Spike is a bit delusional, we recognize and can identify with his mental process.

Animated Cacti

One of the most remarkable animation sequences featuring cacti can be found in the Walt Disney feature film *The Three Caballeros* of 1944, directed by Norman Ferguson. This animation is one of Disney's 'package films' – essentially a collection of disparate animated sequences. One of these involves a choreographed dance sequence that features a live-action Mexican woman, Carmen Molina, and an animated Donald Duck, plus dozens of animated cacti that incessantly change their form as they dance around.

At the start of the sequence, Donald finds himself among a group of cacti that begin to dance and transform. Soon, one of the dancing saguaros turns into a live-action Molina. Donald is immediately enamoured of her, and in an effort to 'fit in' he attempts to strike a cactus-like pose – first as a saguaro, then as an *Opuntia*; but these transformative efforts fail to impress her. He continues to pursue her by emulating her dance movements, but even this gains only a brief acknowledgement by Miss Molina. He then attempts to adopt her Latino-style appearance by transforming his sailor's hat into an enormous sombrero, but that does not impress her much either. Soon, however, the animated cacti actively begin to thwart him in his pursuit of her. They block his way and seem to taunt him – even transforming effortlessly into a flock of perfectly formed cactus-shaped representations of Donald himself, which then proceed to dance painfully on him. In a final effort, Donald races towards Molina, only to have her transform back into a saguaro cactus just as he is about to throw his arms around her; instead, he slams painfully into her spiky trunk.

The animation writer Jay P. Telotte suggests that in this animated sequence the dance between Donald, the cacti and the live-action woman represents not only an immediate frustration for Donald – he does not get the girl – but a much more complex one: he is unable to bridge the genetic and cultural boundaries between cartoon duck and live-action woman.[12] The dancing cacti, though, seem to have no trouble shifting between species and forms as they quickly meta-morphose; and in doing this, the animated cacti actually showcase many of the wide range of forms that real-world cacti can take. This ever-shifting idea of what a 'cactus' actually looks like is in a sense the very embodiment of how differently cacti have been viewed in various societies.

The Evil Cactus

Anthropomorphism can be used to emphasize particular traits inher-ent to the object. In the case of the cactus plant, this can include its menacing spines and strange appearance, effectively forming the basis of an evil or outlawed character.

In the 1890s Joe Mulhatton of Arizona became known for his 'horrific discovery' of a group of 'supernatural' saguaro cacti, as recounted in the local newspapers. He claimed that the saguaros around his property had become heavily 'magnetized' (and essentially animated) owing to huge veins of magnetically charged copper that existed deep underground in the area. These magnetized cacti were allegedly lethal and, depending on their magnetic polarity, would either attract or repel living creatures with enormous force. On one occasion Mulhatton claimed to have witnessed two tramps who were travelling through the desert:

> One of the men was at once drawn up to and impaled on the sharp blades of the cactus, while the octopus-like arms folded around him crushing him through and into the cactus, where his blood, flesh and bones turned into a pulp very much like ordinary mucilage, which trickled out slowly from the aperture made by the passing in of the man's body. The cactus loses its magnetic power while it is digesting its victim. So we were enabled to look at this wonderful yet gruesome sight and report these particulars . . . A negative cactus repelled the second tramp and heaved his body about 100 feet against a positive one, whereupon he met the same fate.[13]

It appears that this story was believed widely, having tapped into the readership's general dislike of cacti. Such a perception was quite at odds with the native peoples' legends of the saguaro – for them it provided essential food for both humans and animals, as well as shelter for many desert creatures.

During the escalation of the Cold War, Hollywood churned out an endless stream of horror films and killer insect movies, such as *The Deadly Mantis* (directed by Nathan Juran, 1957), which seemed to reflect the generalized fear of 'the enemy' that was brewing in American society – the ever-present threat of communism and nuclear war. Comic books also revelled in this type of story, and one classic example of a killer cactus can be found in the *Fantastic Fears* series from Ajax Comics that featured a story titled 'Green Horror' (1954). The story begins with a man and a woman travelling home through the desert. On the way the woman stops so that she can collect a small cutting from a saguaro cactus, in the expectation that it will grow well in her front garden. It does grow and, amazingly, seems to reach its full towering height in just a few months. But the husband soon develops a strong dislike for the cactus, and one day

'Green Horror' tale in an issue of the comic book *Fantastic Fears* (July–August 1954).

he attacks it with an axe. To his horror, the plant comes to life, grabs the axe from him and kills him instantly. A few months after her husband's tragic demise, the woman meets another man, but it seems that in the meantime the cactus has fallen in love with her. Foolishly, the new man proposes to her right in front of the killer cactus. The woman, of course, says yes; while she is inside the house making celebration cocktails, the cactus strikes, pummelling and strangling her new fiancé to death. It then uproots itself and walks to the front door; when the woman opens the door it grabs her, pulls her into a 'loving' embrace and crushes her to death.[14]

Also in the early 1950s, a popular serialized story entitled 'The Monster in Hyde Park' ran in the British youth weekly *The Wizard*. It featured a killer cactus that had set up residence in the famous London park. This giant barrel cactus, which quickly grows to nearly 150 m (500 ft) tall and 1 km (more than ½ mile) wide, is covered in deadly red spines that can be hurled by it over great distances. Even the slightest scratch from these poisonous spines will kill a person. When particularly aggravated, the cactus unfurls one of its ridges, then flicks it outwards 'like something on a spring, but with such force and speed that it hurled loose all the spines that covered its surface'. Such strikes inflict terrible carnage:

> Men tottered about the road, clawing at spines that had pierced their bodies, and crying out to those who had not been pierced to help them. But most of those who appeared unharmed had been scratched by passing spines, and that meant they would share the same fate as their comrades.[15]

Like with the Australian prickly pear infestation, this cactus also propagates and spreads at an alarming rate: 'The dreaded cactus plants were steadily spreading outwards into the outskirts of London, and even beyond. Two had been reported already at Maidenhead.' Drawing blatantly from Australia's prickly pear narrative, the Londoners are finally able to fight back when they discover a mysterious black butterfly whose larvae swiftly devour the cactus's flesh.

There have been many other examples of cactus villains in comics and animated films. In the Marvel Comics *West Coast Avengers* series, a character known simply as Cactus is essentially a giant saguaro (with a somewhat obscured human face) that exhibits great strength, can fly through the air and sprays needles at his victims.

His weakness, however, derives from his high water content – being a succulent plant, he is somewhat fragile and can be easily smashed. But to counteract this perceived weakness, he can instantly regenerate his destroyed body, making him effectively immortal.[16]

In the animated feature film *The Elm-chanted Forest* (directed by Milan Blažeković, 1986), an evil cactus king known as Emperor Spine rules the kingdom; he is a cruel tyrant who wants to turn the beautiful forest into a desert. In the end, he is tricked into drinking a magic potion, which transforms him from a green, spiky cactus into a pink, spine-free flowering plant. To complement his new look, he becomes a kind and benevolent ruler.

Even the long-running British television series *Doctor Who* has featured cactaceous villains. In one memorable four-part episode from 1980, a frightening cactus creature named Meglos becomes the Doctor's nemesis. This giant cactus is apparently the sole survivor of a newly dead and desolate planet: 'I am Meglos, only survivor of this planet. I am a plant! A xerophyte, to be precise!' Meglos appears as a giant potted cactus that, although capable of speech, is unable to move on its own. It does, however, develop the ability to transfer its 'being' into a human form with the aid of a special machine. The machine comprises two compartments, one in which the cactus sits, the other for its human victim. When the transfer takes place, the giant cactus becomes noticeably withered and the human becomes green and covered in cactus spines. Meglos then uses the cactus-human to do its evil bidding. In an interview, the writers of the show described how the inspiration for the Meglos character came to them. They had been sitting around a kitchen table trying to devise the ultimate villain, and it just so happened that in the middle of the table sat a rather 'ugly' cactus plant. At one point they both fixated on the cactus and straight away began developing the Meglos character.[17]

A notable anthropomorphic cactus character, who is unfortunately mistaken for a villain, appeared in a British advertising campaign for the bottled fruit drink Oasis in 2008. The television advertisements chronicle the story of a young woman and her boyfriend,

'Meglos', episode of *Doctor Who* from 1980.

Cactus Kid, who are on the run from the law on the U.S./Mexico border. Cactus Kid is a strange-looking character, performed by a human actor who has been painted green and covered in spines. The tongue-in-cheek adverts explain that because he is a cactus, he 'hates water and only drinks Oasis'. The two manage to stay one step ahead of the police, but the woman is pregnant and soon gives birth to a 'cactus baby'. Eventually the law does catch up with them, and, in different versions of the advert, either they are both shot dead by the police (but the baby survives) or a kindly officer (who also drinks Oasis) allows them to escape with their baby.

Surprisingly, these advertisements were formally banned in the United Kingdom, and two principal reasons were given for the censorship: the storyline was deemed to condone teenage pregnancy, and the oft-repeated slogan 'Oasis: for people who don't like water' was 'irresponsible and could discourage good dietary practice'.[18] The second claim in particular is very unexpected since the advertisements appear merely to be a light-hearted treatment of the fact that cacti, being succulent plants, deal with water somewhat differently from many other plants. In the campaign this was amusingly translated to suggest that they 'don't like water'. As with the undue prejudice that was bestowed upon Cactus Kid in the advertisement narratives, one could wonder if the public's personal bias against cacti might have held some subliminal sway in the judgement of these advertising campaigns. It does seem that cacti, because of their spines, strange appearance and odd behaviour, are rather misunderstood.

Over the past few decades the popularity of cacti has increased in a number of Asian countries; the plant also seems to have gained a more visible presence in Asian popular culture, including, of course, its personification. The anime series *Digimon* features a cactus character named Togemon – a name apparently derived from the word

The evil Meglos, a cactus-like alien, takes the form of a human in the *Doctor Who* episode 'Meglos', 1980.

A television advertisement for Oasis brand drinks, featuring 'Cactus Kid', 2008.

'thorn' – and draws its inspiration from the Easter cactus (*Echinopsis oxygona*). Togemon is an enormous creature that wears large red boxing gloves and is a proficient fighter. But when things get too tough, or if he is up against a particularly difficult opponent, he has the capacity to spray out an array of needles. Other notable animated cactus characters are to be found in the Japanese series *Pokemon*, *Mon Colle Knights* and the *Final Fantasy* video-game and animation franchise. The capacity to spray deadly needles seems to be a common trait among these cactus-inspired characters.

Cactomorphism

The idea of anthropomorphism can be inverted so that, instead of applying human characteristics to a cactus, one can apply cactus characteristics to something else. We can coin the term 'cactomorphism' to describe this inverted condition – where everyday things or creatures are imbued with cactaceous attributes while maintaining their underlying identity.

An example of cactomorphic characters can be found in the highly popular tokidoki brand, a diverse fashion and toy label conceived and designed by the Italian artist Simone Legno. The designs and characters all closely mimic contemporary Japanese styles and have become extremely popular worldwide. One of the more popular

Togemon, from the sixth episode of *Digimon: Digital Monsters*, 1999.

offshoots of this label is the characters and toys that make up the tokidoki *Cactus Friends* series: figurines of small children and their pet kittens and puppies that wear cactus costumes. Although they look a bit like anthropomorphic cacti, it is more precise to describe them as cactomorphic children and animals, since they dress up as cacti, rather than being cacti that look human. The typical Japanese-style super-cute characters from the tokidoki designer range have effect-ively transformed the cactus plant into an equally adorable form. The character description for these creatures reads as follows:

> The cactus is a sign of protection. Kids are naïve and vul-
> nerable and need protection. Sandy and her friends zip
> themselves into cactus suits because they think the world is
> a cold and scary place, and they need some armor to face it.[19]

Of course, these delightful creatures are not threatening at all — but they do show some of the more menacing traits of the cactus plant,

Tokidoki, 'Cactus Friends' collectible figurine series.

Cactus-themed Nativity scenes.

such as the spines, which in this case are not the enemy of man, but rather the protector of human vulnerability.

Another intriguing example of cactomorphism can be found in a series of Halloween decorations that became very popular in the southwest United States, particularly Arizona, in the 1990s. These decorations successfully combined the characteristics of a saguaro cactus (its columnar shape with 'arms') with that of a jack-o'-lantern. Made of blow-mould foam and illuminated by an interior light bulb, they were essentially orange jack-o'-lanterns that had been elongated into the upright forms of saguaro cacti.

In recent years a range of Latin American-produced Christmas nativity scenes, most commonly from Peru and Mexico, have incorporated the cactus in a unique way. Quite a few different styles have been produced over the years, but what they all seem to have in common is that, instead of being set in the usual barn or stable, the miniature figures of Mary, Joseph, the baby Jesus and the visiting shepherds are inside a large cactus form. Thus, rather than simply adding a few cactus plants to the staging of the traditional nativity scene – which would have effectively given local flavour to the scene – the entire Christmas story becomes seamlessly amalgamated into the form and narrative of the cactus. Several different species of cactus have been used in these depictions of the nativity, including the iconic saguaro and the prickly pear.

five

Eating Cacti

❧

The prospect of eating cacti might initially bring to mind spectacles of painful spines piercing the tongue – and, if you do a quick Internet search, you will find countless video postings that feature the outrageous stunt of eating an entire cactus plant, even the spines. It is very unsettling, to say the least, to watch someone take bite after bite from a spiny cactus and then painfully choke down the spines. This extreme stunt may seem novel, but it has actually been performed over centuries. In Europe in the mid-nineteenth century a troupe of Algerian stunt performers became notorious for their daredevil acts; as one of their highlights, each performer would eat an entire cactus stem, spines and all. A newspaper article of 1867 describes a performer as having quickly 'devoured a branch of cactus, the thorns of which pierced his tongue through and through'.[1]

Cacti can in fact be a very good ingredient in cuisine, and almost every part – barring the spines – has been a regular part of human nourishment for thousands of years, from fruit and flowers to stems and roots. Ever since humanity first populated the American continents, people have been consuming these plants. Most cactus fruits and flowers are edible and, although not all cactus species' flesh is suitable to eat (some can be quite indigestible), many make extremely nutritious vegetable dishes.

One of the historic impediments to the wider international acceptance of cacti in cuisine is the negative attitude that many people still hold towards the plants. Cactus just does not sound very appetizing. And it appears that those who are the least familiar with cacti harbour the strongest resistance. Interestingly, the early Jesuit missionaries working in the Americas often tried to discourage the indigenous peoples from eating the plants. Because they had witnessed the mind-altering effect of the peyote cactus on those who consumed it, they seemed to be generally suspicious of most cacti. Even the highly nutritious (and delicious) fruit of numerous columnar cacti were suspected to be 'heathen' in nature. The priests became greatly dismayed when they observed the indigenous people 'sneaking off' to gorge themselves on the ripe fruit; from their perspective, the 'natives' had become hopelessly addicted to it.[2]

In contemporary times, however, the eating of cacti, in particular the fruit, seems to be gaining global popularity. In order to reach a wider market, some growers of cactus fruit have attempted to down-play its cactaceous identity. Some people already regularly eat one very popular fruit, not realizing that it derives from a cactus: dragon fruit. This widely consumed tropical fruit from Vietnam and other Asian countries is actually the fruit of an epiphytic cactus (*Hylocereus*

Varieties of prickly pear fruit.

undatus) that originated in the forested areas of Mexico. There is also mounting evidence that the fruit, stems and flowers of many cacti, particularly those of the *Opuntia* genus, are extremely nutritious and bring many health benefits. As a crop, most cacti are extremely easy to grow, and some people believe that the plants may offer a sustainable alternative to other agricultural crops.

Fruit

Most cactus fruits are edible. Some are fairly bland, rather like a flavourless melon; others are very sweet and juicy; a few can be relatively sour. Some cactus fruits are covered in spines and some with glochids; some are completely smooth-skinned. Technically, all are berries, so they tend to have a large number of seeds enclosed in their fleshy pulp. These seeds range from minute ones the size of poppy seeds to somewhat bigger ones the size of large grape pips. They are edible, and are normally chewed or swallowed along with the fresh

Prickly pear fruit.

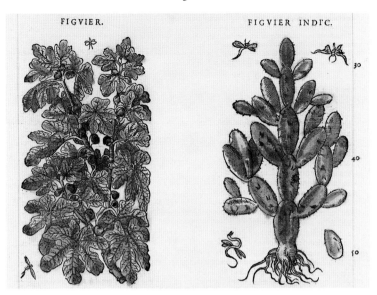

This hand-coloured print by Pietro Andrea Mattioli from 1572 offers a side-by-side comparison of a European fig tree and the 'Indian fig', *Opuntia ficus-indica*, the most commonly eaten variety of prickly pear cactus.

fruit. The larger seeds can be extracted and have traditionally been either toasted and eaten as a snack, or ground into flour.

Perhaps the most widely eaten cactus fruit comes from the prickly pear, which the indigenous people of the Americas have eaten for thousands of years. It is a sweet and nutritious fruit that comes in a variety of colours – usually with red, orange or yellow pulp – and contains numerous black seeds. The fruit can also be made into juice, jam, syrup and even wine. The most popular variety today is *Opuntia ficus-indica*, the Indian fig, originally named by Europeans for the fruit's resemblance to the European fig. The Mexicans refer to the fruit as *tunas*; the most common English name is prickly pear fruit, although in some places it is known as cactus pear – perhaps intending to downplay its 'prickly' nature.

The one major shortcoming of the fruit is that it is normally covered in glochids, those small, almost invisible barbed spines. These must be carefully removed before the fruit is peeled. Increasingly, they are removed mechanically before the fruit is sold. However, if they are not, or if one is harvesting the fruit oneself, great care must be taken. The fruit should be picked using tongs and dropped into a bag or bucket; then should be placed in a sink of water and individually scrubbed to free them of their spines. An abrasive sponge or small scrubbing brush can be used, and gloves should be worn. After scrubbing, it is a good idea to rinse the fruit again under running water. Some people go to more extreme measures and use a portable gas torch to burn off the spines, quickly torching the entire fruit on all sides. Once the spines are removed, it is safe to peel the fruit, and it can be enjoyed raw or cooked.

These cactus fruits are extremely nutritious, containing high levels of calcium, magnesium and potassium as well as abundant amounts of antioxidants.[3] Because the fruit is high in sugar, it makes excellent syrups and jams, and in Mexico it is also used to colour and sweeten drinks and sweets.[4] A novel dessert dish made from the fruit is *queso de tuna* or prickly pear cheese, a solid, brownish or cream-coloured block that resembles a sweet buttery fruit taffy. To make it, the seeds are removed and the pulp is boiled for several hours; it is then cooled while being stirred continuously to prevent it from crystallizing.[5]

Prickly pears – principally O. *ficus-indica* – have been grown commercially for centuries. As we have seen, at the turn of the twentieth century Luther Burbank became known for his 'spineless' variety of O. *ficus-indica*, and marketed it heavily. Others have continued his work, and most commercial crops are now spineless; however, the pads and fruit still contain some glochids. The major producing countries are Mexico, Italy, South Africa, Tunisia, Chile, Argentina and the United States. Mexico, with more than 70,000 ha (173,000 acres), generates some 50 per cent of the world's production. Sicily comes in second, with more than 18,000 ha (45,000 acres).[6] A number of other countries have smaller, albeit rapidly increasing, yields. Many see it as a good crop to grow in more arid climates, and it can usually be grown without irrigation.[7] Undeniably, world demand for the fruit is skyrocketing.

Auguste Renoir, *Still-life with Flowers and Prickly Pears*, c. 1885, oil on canvas.

The fruit grows around the top edges of the pads or cladodes. Anything from three to twenty fruit may grow on each cladode, but they are normally thinned to promote the larger growth of the remaining fruit.[8] An oft-repeated story tells of a Sicilian farmer who became furious with his neighbour after the neighbour's son made advances towards his daughter. In retribution, one night he sabotaged his neighbour's cactus crop, knocking off all the flower buds from his prickly pear plants. To his dismay, the plants quickly regrew new

Prickly pear fruit.

flowers, and went on to produce an abundant crop of exceptionally large fruit.[9] The practice of systematically removing the initial flower buds proved to be such an effective agricultural strategy that it soon became a regular farming practice throughout Sicily, and was even given a name, *scozzolatura*.[10]

Perhaps the second most popular cactus fruit, and one that is rising quickly in popularity, is that of the dragon fruit, pitaya or pitahaya, *Hylocereus undatus*. It is primarily an epiphytic cactus, or more accurately hemi-epiphytic, and grows naturally on tree branches in the tropical areas of Mexico and Central America. It was brought to Vietnam by the French in 1860 and was originally grown in limited quantities, primarily reserved for the upper classes. In recent decades it has become a major agricultural crop; it is consumed locally, and is increasingly exported around the world. As an agricultural crop, these climbing cacti are normally grown with the aid of tall support posts. The fruit and stems are allowed to spill over the tops of the posts and hang down almost to the ground. It is a highly prolific crop, and plantations can produce several harvests each year.

Dragon fruit, also known as pitaya.

The dragon fruit has become so common and entrenched in Vietnamese culture that many assume it to be a tropical fruit that is native to the region, never imagining it actually to be a Mexican cactus. It has even developed its own local mythology, which claims that the fruit originated from the mouths of fire-breathing dragons. In battle, after a dragon was slain, the fruit would be collected and presented as proof that the dragon had been defeated.[11] Although Vietnam is its major producer, the fruit is increasingly grown in many other Asian countries, as well as Australia, South Africa, Israel (where it is sometimes referred to as Eden fruit) and South America.

The fruit is free of spines and can easily reach a hefty 500 g (1 lb) or more. Many people have compared its consistency to a kiwi fruit – both its pulp and its seeds. Although it is juicy, its flavour is fairly mild and melon-like. The fruit is very striking in appearance, normally red on the outside and with white pulp, although other related varieties of *Hylocereus* are becoming more common – with yellow, red or even purple pulp.

The best-tasting fruit can be found growing on some of the tallest columnar cacti, particularly those belonging to the *Stenocereus* genus. These have historically been available commercially only in South America and Mexico, but they are beginning to be introduced elsewhere. A number of growers of dragon fruit and prickly pear are also beginning to grow limited quantities of columnar cactus fruit.

There are many different varieties of columnar cactus fruit. Some are small, about the size of a grape; others as big as a large apple. Some have ordinary spines, some long, soft, hair-like spines, and many no spines at all, but any spines tend to be fairly large and can be removed easily without fear of ingesting them. The peel of the fruit can be green, orange, red or bright pink. The pulp usually looks similar to that of the dragon fruit and is normally white, yellow or red in colour, with numerous small seeds. A mature plant can produce vast quantities of fruit and, since the fruit tends to split open as it ripens, it must be harvested before it becomes too ripe.

Perhaps the most famous and widely studied fruit-producing columnar cactus is the saguaro (*Carnegiea gigantea*), which the indigenous Tohono O'odham people of the Sonoran Desert have been eating for centuries. Again, the fruit bursts open when ripe, and from a distance can look like a bright red flower. To collect the fruit, the harvester knocks it from the plant with a long pole, made from the timber ribs from dead saguaros. It is eaten fresh and used to make jam and wine, and the seeds are ground into meal to make flatbread. Following each harvest, the Tohono O'odham conduct an elaborate, festive winemaking ritual that forms part of their annual ceremony to ensure adequate rainfall during the coming year.[12]

Pereskia aculeata, which has leaves and in fact looks nothing like a cactus, produces small orange berries, commonly known as Barbados gooseberries, that can be found in local markets throughout the West Indies. These are commonly made into jam or baked into pies. A number of barrel cactus fruit, such as those of *Ferocactus histrix* (the *biznaga* cactus), are eaten regularly and sold throughout Mexico. These fruit are commonly called *tuna de biznaga* and sometimes *borrachitos* ('little drunk men'), since the fruit is sometimes fermented to make an alcoholic drink.[13]

Most cacti also have edible flowers, which are widely consumed – particularly those of the prickly pear. These have been likened to rose hips and hibiscus flowers in flavour and usage, and can be eaten raw, or dried and used to make tea.[14] The floral buds of the *biznaga* cactus are commonly called *cabuches* and are sold commercially, both fresh and canned, in Mexico. They can be added to soups or to fried eggs.[15] The Tohono O'odham have traditionally eaten the buds of the cholla cactus. These are normally cooked and added to soups, stews or salads; they are very rich in calcium.[16]

Cactus Vegetables

Several varieties of cactus can be eaten as a vegetable, but those most commonly consumed in this way are the pads (cladodes) of

The inside of a dragon fruit.

the prickly pear, known in Spanish as *nopal*. The youngest, darkest green cladodes are the most tender and delicious. Even though it is primarily the spineless variety that is consumed, the pads can still be covered with glochids and must be handled carefully. Using tongs, the small pads can easily be twisted off the plant. Prickly pear cacti are a CAM (crassulacean acid metabolism; see Chapter One) plant, so the pads are usually picked in the late afternoon; they taste slightly bitter (acidic) if picked in the morning, owing to an overnight build-up of malic acid (stored CO_2). As with the fruit, they must be scrubbed

Red-fleshed dragon fruit, considered by many to be the most flavourful variety.

Cactus laden with brightly coloured pitaya.

carefully under running water with an abrasive sponge or scrubbing brush. Once the glochids are removed, the outer edges should be trimmed; the pads can then be sliced into strips. They can be eaten raw or cooked, but normally it is a good idea at least to boil them lightly so as to remove some of the mucilage, which can give the cactus flesh a slightly slimy texture.

The pads can also be pickled with vinegar, spices, onions and other vegetables. They can be made into savoury sauces, or into marmalade, jam or confectionery, or dried, ground and added to flour for baking.[17] They are extremely nutritious and, surprisingly, they contain the full array of amino acids – including eight that cannot be manufactured by the human body.[18] They are also moderately high in antioxidants, including vitamins A and C. Recent studies have confirmed that they have anti-diabetic properties and can therefore be useful in the treatment of many forms of this condition.[19]

The flesh of some varieties of barrel cactus, such as the *biznaga* cactus, has proven edible. The pulp is scooped out and either boiled or fried, often with sugar, to produce a sweetmeat that can be eaten as a confection, or mixed into tamales and other semi-savoury dishes.[20]

Pereskia aculeata with its edible (and highly nutritious) leaves.

A Native American woman harvesting the fruit of the saguaro cactus, *c.* 1907.

This pulp is the source of the 'cactus candy' treats that were widely available in shops in the southwestern United States throughout the later twentieth century. The native peoples of the Netherlands Antilles, now in the Dutch Caribbean, regularly eat *Cereus repandus*, a tall columnar cactus. With the skin removed, this cactus is sliced and boiled or fried, then made into soups and other savoury dishes. In South America, the small globular cactus *Neowerdermannia vorwerkii* is skinned and eaten like a potato by the indigenous peoples of Bolivia.[21]

Cacti fruit (pitaya) from a columnar cactus.

Cactus salad, containing *Pereskia aculeata* cactus leaves, red *Disocactus* flower petals, tomato and cheese.

Peniocereus greggii, the night-blooming cereus or queen of the night, is a very thin, spiny cactus. In particularly arid conditions the plants can appear withered, brown and lifeless, their spindly stems sprawling over rocks and up the trunks of larger plants. Because the plant's stem has very limited succulence, it stores most of its moisture in a large, tuberous root that resembles a turnip. Also like turnips, these roots are edible and can be baked, or cut into strips and fried. The tubers can grow quite large: one unusually big specimen was found to weigh nearly 45 kg (100 lb).[22]

The leaves of *Pereskia aculeata* can be eaten raw or cooked; this cactus is popular in Brazil, where it is known colloquially as *ora-pro-nobis*, literally 'pray for us'. In the United States, it is sometimes called sweet Mary or, referring to its fruit, Barbados gooseberry or Spanish gooseberry. The leaves have a gentle flavour reminiscent of spinach leaves and, like spinach, are lightly boiled and eaten as a vegetable side dish or used as an ingredient in other dishes, soups and salads. Surprisingly, it has emerged from recent studies that the leaves are extremely high in protein – calculated at between 20 and 25 per cent (weight for weight), which is higher than that of most beans.

Importantly, this protein is also very high in essential amino acids, including lysine. The leaves contain high levels of many minerals, including calcium, potassium, manganese, zinc and iron.[23] But while in some places (Australia, parts of the United States and particularly South Africa) this plant has become a very troublesome weed, in the light of recent and emerging studies of its nutritional value it is becoming increasingly valued as a nutritional supplement.

Cactus Medicine

In addition to providing sustenance, cacti have for thousands of years been used extensively in traditional medicine by indigenous peoples of North and South America for pain relief and antibacterial treatments, and to relieve stomach disorders, ear infections, heart and kidney ailments and skin problems, among other uses.[24] The Aztecs used the prickly pear cactus to cleanse the digestive system and eliminate intestinal worms; eating it was also thought to strengthen the heart and lungs, and even to increase lactation during breastfeeding.[25]

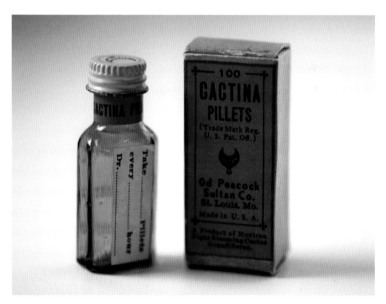

Cactina Pillets, produced by the Sultan Drug Co. from *c.* 1890–1940.

In the late nineteenth century an Italian physician discovered that the flesh of *Selenicereus grandiflorus*, a thin-stemmed epiphytic night-blooming cactus, possessed therapeutic properties.[26] Within a few years the Sultan Drug Co. of St Louis, Missouri, and London began producing Cactina Pillets, a medication derived from the cactus. These very small tablets or pillets were described as being 'a product of the Mexican night-blooming cactus'. Each contained the very vaguely stated ingredient: 'One one-hundredth of a grain of Cactina – the active proximate principle of Cactus Mexicana.' These Cactina Pillets were marketed primarily as a remedy for a 'weak heart', but were also prescribed as general medication for the '*collateral treatment* in febrile, nervous, uterine, and other diseases'. The pills were promoted heavily, and one edition of the company's frequent newsletter stated: 'It is but natural that any remedy that regulates the pumping properties of the heart, without any harmful effects, will regulate the circulation and improve general nutrition. Cactina Pillets is that remedy.'[27] As was the case with many tonics of the day, the claims, while grandiose, were entirely vague. The central claim for the pillets was that they would improve the heart, but with each new promotional pamphlet they were increasingly purported to treat almost every ailment imaginable. They cost 25 cents per 100 pillets in 1892, and at this price the suggested dosage also seemed opportunely frequent: 'One Pillet every hour, or every two hours, as may be necessary.'

More recently, prickly pear pads have been used to treat many different conditions, most notably diabetes (as a supplementary treatment), and there are now countless products that include them, labelled either as nopal or prickly pear. As a nutritional supplement prickly pear can be purchased in powder form and as capsules, tea or as an ingredient in various other drinks. Nopal biscuits, cookies, health bars – and just about any other product one could imagine – are also becoming widely available. Although there is compelling evidence that demonstrates the important health benefits of the prickly pear, one might wonder if, like the Sultan Drug Co. and its

Cactina Pillets, some manufacturers might be slightly overselling this 'amazing super-food'.

A few cactus species are known to contain moderate levels of mescaline and other related alkaloids, which can provoke an intoxicating and psychoactive effect in humans. The two most notable are the peyote cactus (*Lophophora williamsii*) and the San Pedro cactus (*Trichocereus pachanoi*). It is believed that these chemicals serve as a natural defence for the cacti: in lieu of spines, they have high concentrations of chemicals in their flesh, which animals find distasteful and so avoid eating. Yet it is remarkable how profoundly these chemicals seem to affect the human neurological system. The consumption of these cacti, mainly as part of religious rituals, goes back thousands of years. However, in addition to having psychoactive properties, the peyote cactus has been used in traditional medicine to treat extreme pain and to aid in difficult childbirth. Similarly, the San Pedro cactus has recently been used to treat alcoholism and ailments of the stomach, liver and kidneys.[28]

The peyote, the most recognized of the alkaloid-containing cacti, is a small, spineless cactus that is native to the Chihuahuan Desert of northern Mexico and parts of Texas. It has, however, been cultivated over a much wider area and used for both religious and medical purposes for thousands of years (dating back as early as 7,000 years ago).[29] Since this diminutive cactus has no spines, it must use other, more ingenious methods to discourage animals from eating it. One is camouflage: it produces small, globular, offset 'buttons' that grow on top of one another. To passing animals, it looks rather like piles of dung. It also stores much of its moisture underground in a large, tuberous taproot, difficult for a thirsty animal to access. The final defence is its strong alkaloid content, which animals find very unpleasant. It is this alkaloid, comprising mescaline and a number of other chemicals, that produces a mind-altering effect in humans. But peyote does not actually cause hallucinations; it often causes one to see extremely vivid colours and intricate patterns, and enhances the senses. On first consuming the cactus, one experiences intense

San Pedro cactus,
Trichocereus pachanoi.

nausea, vomiting and dizziness, which are followed by the 'high' or 'psychic intoxication'.[30] Early Jesuit priests called peyote the Devil's root (*raíz diabolica*) and tried their best to discourage its use by native peoples. In some cases, converts to Catholicism would combine the traditional use of peyote with their Christian religion.[31] Several native tribes in Mexico still use peyote regularly as an important part of their religious rituals. In the mid-nineteenth century its use had spread north into the United States, and by the twentieth century nearly 300,000 Native Americans there had become members of the Native American Church, in which the peyote cactus is still eaten as part of its religious sacrament.[32]

The tall columnar San Pedro cactus is similar in effect to peyote, although some claim it to be much less potent. Ancient stone carvings of figures holding up pieces of this cactus have been found at the ruins of the temple of Chavín de Huántar in the mountains of Peru, indicating that humans have been consuming it for at least 3,000 years. Many other ancient carvings, ceramics and imagery have been found that appear to pay homage to the cactus. Its use was also greatly discouraged by the Catholic Church, but some groups effectively blended the traditional uses of this plant with Catholicism, and that is probably how it came to be known by the decidedly Spanish Catholic name of San Pedro.[33] As with peyote, its consumption is usually followed by very intense nausea and vomiting.

A number of artists and literary figures were known for their use of peyote. Perhaps most notable was Aldous Huxley, author of the chilling novel *Brave New World* (1932). He wrote several of his novels while under the influence of mescaline, and his book *The Doors*

Peyote cactus, *Lophophora williamsii*.

of Perception (1954) explicitly highlights the effects of peyote. Later, William S. Burroughs and subsequent Beat authors such as Jack Kerouac and Allen Ginsberg were also said to have experimented with this alkaloid.

Many people have suggested that the use of these plants will remain marginal as they require a great deal of dedication: one has first to endure a very intense sickness before any intoxicating effects manifest themselves. The law regulating the use of these plants seems to change frequently, and can vary dramatically from one jurisdiction to the next. In the United States and Mexico it is illegal to possess, grow or consume peyote – unless one is an official member of the Native American Church, in which case there are some legal exceptions. In other countries there may be no regulation at all. The San Pedro cactus is generally considered to be less potent, and because it is so pervasive as a common garden plant, most localities do not impose very severe restrictions. In some areas it is permissible to grow the plant, but illegal to ingest it or to extract the alkaloids.

In 2011 in Australia, there was a push to criminalize the growing of all cacti and other plants that contain mescaline (and many other similar chemicals). It was found, however, that a number of species of cactus could contain at least trace amounts of these chemicals. Even a few species of the prickly pear, one of the most widespread cacti in the world, may contain minute amounts – although it is estimated that one would have to eat many kilograms (essentially a truckload) to get even the most negligible psychoactive effect. Further complicating this proposed legislation, it emerged that there are many hundreds of other species of cactus that have never been tested to determine their chemical make-up. The result of this proposal would be that at some point in the future hundreds of other species of cactus could suddenly be designated illegal. Even more troublesome, it has been found that such chemicals are prevalent far beyond the cactus family; these and similar chemicals are rampant in large sections of the plant kingdom, including many native Australian plants. As the details of the proposed legislation became known, a groundswell of opposition mounted, and it was eventually abandoned.[34] But the proposals did highlight just how widespread these naturally occurring chemicals are in the plant kingdom.

Livestock Feed

Humans are not, of course, the only ones who eat cacti. The prickly pear (*Opuntia ficus-indica*) in particular has been found to be an important source of forage and fodder for domesticated animals (cattle, sheep, goats and pigs). The pads provide a substantial reserve of energy, vitamins and minerals, some protein and, importantly, water. The high water content makes the cactus an ideal food in arid regions – it has, in fact, been found that if sheep are fed the pads they will require no drinking water at all. Nevertheless, because of its relatively low levels of protein, phosphorous and sodium compared to many grains, some supplemental feed is usually required.[35]

Generally, the spineless variety of prickly pear is the most widely used as livestock feed, although various spiny varieties have also been used effectively. In some areas, particularly in parts of Texas, the spines are singed off entire fields of prickly pear whenever a new source of food is needed. When the spines are intact the cattle will not touch the cacti, eating just the grass around them, but they eagerly devour them once the spines have been removed, a strategy that can effectively preserve the feed source until it is needed most.[36] Its use as a livestock feed has been increasing rapidly in recent decades. Currently the three largest growers of *O. ficus-indica* for fodder are Tunisia (which has more than 500,000 ha/1.2 million acres in cultivation), Brazil (370,000 ha/900,000 acres) and Mexico (230,000 ha/570,000 acres).[37]

six

Transforming the Cactus

To many, the identity of the cactus remains elusive. People have very complex and widely varying views of cacti, and they have perceived and interacted with the plants accordingly. Even within the scientific community, the identity of the cactus has proved to be incredibly fluid as botanists continue to rename and reclassify the cactus family. Various species and genera have been lumped together in recent years; others have been divided into distinct groupings. New species are found periodically, and some that had been considered in the past to be separate species have been determined to be merely variations or hybrids of other species.

But to add to this volatility, cacti themselves are unstable biological forms, and their evolution continues unabated, as a result of both natural causes and, increasingly, human intervention. A number of factors are facilitating this ongoing transformation: cacti are easily cloned, easily grafted, easily hybridized and also easily transmuted. They are indeed very easily transformed organisms, and people seem to be taking increasing advantage of this characteristic.

Hybridizing and Selection

There can be wide differences within a single species of cactus – including variations in shape, texture, spines and flower colour. Growers have sought to exploit these variations, selecting specimens

An illustration of a monstrose cactus, from A. P. de Candolle's *Revue de la famille des cactées*
(1829).

Luther Burbank with his spineless *Opuntia*, c. 1890.

that exhibit particularly desired traits and cross-pollinating them to produce further variations of the species.

Furthermore, cacti are well suited to hybridization. This includes not only the crossing of distinctly different species, but crossbreeding between distinct genera (making them clearly bigeneric plants). Such crosses take place frequently in the wild, resulting in many naturally occurring inter-species and inter-genus hybrids. Even the most popular variety of prickly pear cactus, *Opuntia ficus-indica*, is believed to be a natural hybrid of several different species of *Opuntia*.[1] A number of other wild varieties have been determined to be very complex hybrids, and some of them are, in effect, hybrids of hybrids of hybrids.

In cultivation, hybridization is increasingly used to produce astonishing new forms, such as × *Ferobergia* (the × prefix denoting that it is a cross between species in different genera), a hybrid between *Ferocactus* and *Leuchtenbergia*. These two species are quite distinctive in appearance, and the resulting cross is a striking blend of the two.

One of the most celebrated of the early commercial hybridizers of cacti was Luther Burbank, who, as we have seen, spent many years in the later nineteenth century developing a spineless variety of prickly pear – one that would also produce larger and juicier fruit. He saw great promise in these cacti, envisioning that they would become an important food crop both for animal and human consumption. His breeding efforts were on a very large scale. He would grow hundreds of thousands of hybrid seedlings, select from them and cross them further with other choice specimens through hand-pollination. Although his goal was to create a spine-free *Opuntia*, some of the first hybrids that emerged were actually spinier than their parents. This did not surprise Burbank, since most hybridized plants produce stronger and more vigorous offspring, a condition that is known as hybrid vigour. But he persisted diligently in his selective breeding, and after more than a decade he achieved some very promising results, as a promotional publication by the Luther Burbank Company extolled in 1912:

> The romance and marvel of the Burbank Cactus would fill a large book. The story of the sixteen years of patient effort employed by that wonder-worker, Luther Burbank, justly calls for a place in literature. Imagine, if you please, a man collecting the cacti of the world, selecting from all of these varieties the best, then growing millions of seedlings, crossing and recrossing them, selecting and reselecting and, finally, after sixteen years triumphantly evolving from this patient, laborious process and from millions of discarded cacti, seven plants which were not only free from spines, but which possessed the growing and feeding values for which he had so long striven.[2]

Even Burbank acknowledged that he was not the first to attempt to grow 'spineless' cacti, but what made his efforts so remarkable was the scale on which he worked, the quality of his results and, according to author and cacti expert Gordon Rowley, the fact that 'above all he developed exceptional skill in spotting just those few seedlings out of hundreds or thousands that had potential: a combination of minute observations, experience and intuition.'[3]

Once Burbank had succeeded in producing a few 'perfect' plants – ones that had improved fruit and were truly 'spineless' (although not completely free of glochids) – he set about making thousands of clones. He did so simply by breaking off paddles and planting them, since propagating by seed would not produce identical copies. As another of his promotional catalogues explained:

> [Burbank] cactus should always be raised from cuttings, never under any circumstances from seed, as it always runs back to the thorny kind when grown from seed, but never when grown from cuttings. It has been proved time and time again in thousands and thousands of cases that the new spineless cactus does not run back to the thorny state any more than a Baldwin apple can change to a Ben Davis or a Bartlett pear to a wild pear.[4]

Burbank was a great marketer and very media savvy, and his plants became household names in America. News stories appeared frequently in the press extolling the virtues of his sensational cacti. Until then, most people had considered cacti to be synonymous with spines, yet Burbank's cacti delightfully refuted these firm associations, and seemed to resonate exceptionally well with the public. Countless postcards and promotional materials that celebrated these spine-free cacti were produced for widespread distribution.

Burbank spineless cacti still persist around the world. Clones of his original *Opuntias* are represented in collections, and modern variations are being grown commercially. Currently, a lot of effort is being put into the development of improved cultivars of fruiting cacti, especially prickly pear and dragon fruit, in an attempt to produce larger, sweeter and more flavoursome fruit.

The Art of the Cultivar

There is definitely an art to hybridization and selection, and many new and surprising cultivars are being created continually in the cactus family. Some of the most unusual selective breeding has occurred in the genera *Astrophytum*. This diminutive genus comprises only a handful of species: *Astrophytum asterias*, *A. capricorne*, *A. myriostigma*, *A. ornatum* and the recently discovered species *A. caput-medusae* (found for the first time in 2001). Since most available varieties are spineless, except as seedlings, astrophytums have become very popular; even among those who generally 'do not like cacti', their compact and unusual form has found wide appeal. These species also make excellent subjects for cultivation, and some extraordinary varieties have been produced. Most notable are the cultivars of *A. asterias* that have been produced in Japan, the most famous of which are referred to as 'Super Kabuto'. These are highly regarded and sought after by collectors, and they sell for astronomical prices. The distinguishing feature of these particular cacti is the striking white, fluffy dots that spread across them.

The 'Super Kabuto' was pioneered in Japan by Masaomi Takeo, who found a strange, discoloured variant of *A. asterias* half-dead in a nursery in the United States in 1981. He resuscitated it, and from this plant he and his friend Tony Sato cultivated a unique variety that became 'Super Kabuto'. It was made commercially available in 1983.[5] These cultivars were developed further in Japan and many other countries both by independent hobbyists and by larger nurseries. Some of the plants that have been produced in recent years look almost nothing like the originating wild variety. The plants can have huge variations in the number of ribs (from three to eight), all manner of patterns, ranges of colour and texture, and wide variations in form and flower colour.[6]

Many other notable cultivars have been produced within the epiphytic cacti, particularly the *Schlumbergera* hybrids (often referred to as Christmas cacti), in which special effort has been made to produce varieties with brilliant and long-lasting blooms in a wide range of colours. The orchid cacti, a range of hybrids from the genera *Epiphyllum* and *Disocactus*, have also been cultivated to produce truly remarkable floral displays.

Grafting Cacti

Cacti take very readily to grafting – the fusing of the vascular systems of cuttings from two or more different plants. They also seem to have no problem being grafted on to plants of very different species, genera and even subfamilies.[7]

Probably the most popular forms of grafted cactus are the coloured varieties (red, orange, yellow, purple) of *Gymnocalycium mihanovichii* that are grafted on to upright rootstocks, usually those of *Hylocereus* sp.). These are often referred to as moon cacti or, somewhat pejoratively, as lollipop cacti, since they can look like bright red lollipops on sticks. At first, many have mistaken these bright colourations for flowers, or have assumed that the plants had been injected with a vibrant, but artificial, dye. In fact, they are albino cacti, devoid of the essential green chlorophyll pigmentation, a fact that makes visible any other naturally occurring pigments that they might contain. However, without chlorophyll they cannot carry out photosynthesis, and so they must be grafted onto a green (photosynthetically active) rootstock in order to survive.

These albino cacti originated in Japan from the work of the botanist Eiji Watanabe, who in the late 1930s imported a few hundred *Gymnocalycium* seeds from Germany. From these he produced over 10,000 seedlings, a few of which were mutations, and of these two were distinctly reddish in colour. He developed these further and eventually came up with a bright red albino that he named 'Hibotan'. He also developed other hues, most of which contained some chlorophyll, and dubbed them 'Hibotan Nishiki'.[8] Within a few decades, millions of these plants were being sold each year. Today Korea and, increasingly, China are the major exporters of these cacti.

Most established cactus collectors do not regard these cacti very seriously, for a number of reasons. One is that they look rather artificial and cheap as they sit astride their spindly rootstock. Another reason is perhaps that, since they originated in Japan (a country that was not internationally recognized as being at the forefront of the botanical study of cacti) and at a time when the phrase 'made in Japan' was often synonymous with low-cost, mass-produced items, they became equated with cheap trinkets. An additional reason is that they tend not to be very long-lasting. The rootstock (*Hylocereus*) is essentially a tropical plant, and does not do well in cold weather; also, the growth of the scion (*Gymnocalycium*) seems to stress the fast-growing but insubstantial rootstock. In the care of an inexperienced grower, most such grafted cacti do not last beyond twelve months. Gordon Rowley makes note of this as he hints (rather tongue-in-cheek) at what might be a planned obsolescence: the rootstock 'usually dies off the first winter unless kept extra warm, leaving the customer to crave for a replacement'.[9] It is intriguing, given the current collectors' craze for mutated and unconventional varieties of cactus, that these cacti are still largely dismissed. Some growers, though, routinely graft the plants on to more robust and attractive rootstock. And even though they are not highly regarded by cactus connoisseurs, the plants have proved to be very popular and have served as accessible 'gateway' plants for those new to cacti. Many such owners have gone on to become prodigious cactus enthusiasts.

A slow-growing plant almost always does better when grafted on to a more vigorous rootstock. The bulk of growth hormones originate within the roots of the cacti. These are propelled up to the graft – and with this stronger-than-normal rush of hormones, the scion tends to grow much faster and larger. Thus grafting becomes

Epiphyllum sp. cultivar.

the essential strategy for saving damaged plants and for giving slow-growing specimens a boost. It can also be used to jump-start the growth of seedlings, which are often grafted on to the thin-stemmed *Pereskiopsis*; once they reach a viable size they can be cut off the rootstock, allowed to callus over at the base, and planted into soil.[10]

Occasionally a most remarkable outcome can result from the grafting of two different species of cactus, when, instead of merely existing in a symbiotic relationship, the rootstock and the scion fuse into a single organism. For example, the scion might take on certain very distinctive attributes of the rootstock while maintaining some of its own characteristics. Such remarkable fusions are sometimes referred to as chimera, after the mythical beasts that combined multiple animal forms. These new asexual blends are not hybrids in the traditional sense, so, rather than placing an × in front of the name, a + sign is used to denote that two species have been *added* together. For example, a number of chimera of *Hylocereus* and *Gymnocalycium* have produced + *Hylogymnocalycium*, which Rowley describes as a merger in which *Gymnocalycium* 'Hibotan' 'swallowed its grafting stock, Hylocereus'.[11] Another relatively common example is + *Myrtillocalycium* 'Polyp', a grafted fusion of *Myrtillocactus* and *Gymnocalycium*.[12]

Mutations

Cacti seem very prone to transmutation, and many bizarrely mutated forms have emerged. The reasons for these mutations remain unknown, although a number of theories have been put forward, including general environmental stress, extreme weather, disease, heavy pesticide use, physical trauma and 'genetic drift'. We have not yet learned how to prevent or induce mutations directly, but in recent years we seem to have learned how to select, nurture and rather unnaturally mollycoddle our malformed cacti.

Attitudes towards mutated cacti have changed dramatically over the years. In 1960 Edward Bloom declared that 'untypical or

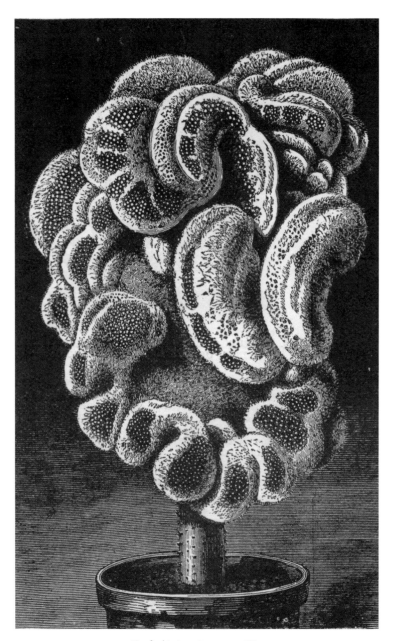

Grafted 'cristate' cactus, c. 1887.

Mammillaria bocasana, a monstrose variety commonly known as 'Fred'.

malformed plants should be avoided; they are never likely to satisfy, and you will spoil the appearance of your collection by harbouring them.'[13] This is in stark contrast to Rowley's more contemporary description:

> There is something uniquely satisfying in picking through a pan of seedlings, and saving just one odd miscreant that most growers would have instinctively discarded. An equal thrill is exploring the thousands of potted seedlings in a large nursery and choosing one oddball, hoping that the vendor doesn't spot the yellow streak or broadening apex and hastily withdraw it from sale.[14]

Of course, not everyone appreciates mutated cacti, but certainly they seem to be growing in popularity. Some collectors no doubt find that after every other species available has been collected, they still desire something else, and so they strive to acquire some of the more unusual variations and mutations. On the current market, mutated cacti generally sell for much higher prices than their conventional (non-mutated) forms.

Mutated cacti can begin to revert to their previous natural, and usually more vigorous, form. New growths or offsets might express none of the monstrose traits of the rest of the plant, as if it is attempting to overcome its mutant malady. Yet, rather than assisting the plant to do so, many growers today do just the opposite, quickly removing any offending normal growths so that the plant remains fully monstrose. In doing so, we are participating in a rather 'unnatural selection' process by helping mutations to continue and to flourish.

The three most common types of cactus mutation are variegates, cristates and monstrose. Variegation has to do with abnormal colouring, while cristation and monstrosity (which are related) have to do with modifications of form.

Variegated cacti, those often displaying streaks of white, yellow, red, orange or purple among the green of the stems, have sections with little or no chlorophyll present. Reverse variegated cacti primarily express one of these colours, displaying only streaks of green. Generally the reverse variegates, and the fully albino cacti, burn easily in the sun and need more care. Since many are less able to conduct photosynthesis, they may need more light, or to be grafted on to a green rootstock.

Crested cacti, also called cristate or fasciated, are mutated or atypical specimens in which the growing tips stop elongating, broadening instead into a malformed spread. These tips tend to fan out into a crest, or sometimes spiral back into irregular folds (as with the brain cactus).

In the wild, the saguaro cactus occasionally mutates, forming an extraordinary crested growth. In the Sonoran Desert, several thousand crested saguaros have been discovered over the years, although that is still a very small percentage of the total saguaro

Variegated cactus, *Ferocactus* sp.

population. They have been celebrated for their unique quality, and more recently have attracted greater protection under the law than their 'normal', non-mutated cousins. In direct contrast to the contemporary interest in mutated cacti, the indigenous peoples of South America have continually avoided eating the fruit from mutated plants, even though the fruit is most probably identical to that from normal plants.[15]

Cristate cacti with one stem (on right) displaying reverted normal growth.

Crested saguaro.

Similar to the crested varieties are the monstrose cacti. These also have mutations that affect the physical form of the cactus, often resulting in asymmetrical growth. Some plants appear gnarled or knobbly, and some lack spines that would usually have them in their non-mutated form. One of the most common is *Pachycereus schottii* var. *monstrosus*, which seems to occur quite frequently in nature. It generally lacks spines, has a gnarled, sculptural look and is commonly referred to as the totem cactus. Another is *Mammillaria bocasana* 'Fred', which in recent years has been heavily cultivated. It also generally lacks spines, and produces very prolific (but small) offshoots that are usually variegated. A third is *Trichocereus bridgesii* 'Monstrosus', which has growth points submerged deep below the surface of its skin, so that when a new stem develops it literally has to burst through the old skin in order to grow – a process that can look painfully unnatural.

Tissue Culture and Genetically Modified Cacti

Tissue culture, or micro-propagation, is a technique that is used to clone plants from very small tissue samples. To create a new plant by tissue culture, only the most minute segment is required – even a

Cristate or crested cacti.

single meristem cell (the cells that contain the information needed to create a new plant) is enough. There is no need to wait for the plant to grow to full size, the point at which vegetative propagation becomes feasible. Generally the meristems are found just below the areoles of the cactus, although in some cases they may be difficult to reach, since they are often protected by spines and wool. Once the cells are removed they are sterilized and placed into a gel solution that provides nutrients and growth hormones. Each meristem soon begins to produce both roots and shoots, usually at an accelerated rate. In this way several hundred clones, if not many thousands, can be produced from a single plant in a very short time.[16]

Although the lollipop cactus (*Gymnocalycium mihanovichii*) tends to produce offsets quickly, propagation by tissue culture has also been

Monstrose cactus, *Trichocereus bridgesii* 'Monstrosus', with new stem growth beginning to burst through its outer skin.

used to create the vast quantities of these cacti that are demanded by the international market. This method can also be used to propagate endangered species, as a means of accelerated off-site cultivation, as well as new speciality hybrids and mutations. This is particularly important when species produce few offsets, have low germination rates, are self-sterile or very slow-growing.[17] As techniques improve and become more accessible, it will probably become the standard, essential method for cactus propagation.

Cacti, like most organisms, can be deliberately modified through the manipulation of genetic material. One interesting experiment to merge artistic and scientific goals was conducted through C-Lab, a group in the United Kingdom that blends art and science to produce 'bio art'. In 2001 the artist Laura Cinti launched what was dubbed 'The Cactus Project', an experiment that introduced keratin genes from human hair into cactus cells. The cacti, quite remarkably, began to grow 'hairs' that undeniably resembled human hair more than the normal cactus hair (trichomes) – although, according to the project summary, some discussion has ensued as to the true nature of the hair, and whether it was really 'human' hair or not.[18] One writer questioned, more philosophically, why one would consider this hair to be human: 'Doesn't it belong now to the cactus and not in a trivial sense either?' To the viewer who experiences this work, it clearly appears as though the hair is being grown and expressed through the cactus.[19] Nonetheless, the project raised a number of interesting questions about the fluctuating identity of cacti, as well as the potential and literal manifestation of anthropomorphism in cacti.

The Amorphous Cactus

As the world continues to grapple with the identity of cacti, the plants themselves persist on their amorphous journey, appearing to transform effortlessly from one permutation to another. Much of this change has occurred naturally, but a substantial amount has occurred through human intervention.

Genetically modified cactus expressing 'human hair', C-Lab, UK.

'Totem Pole' cacti, *Pachycereus schottii* 'monstrose'.

Perhaps we should ask why this occurs, what it is that drives us humans to meddle with cacti in this way. Is it because the cactus plant is an entity that is full of paradox? In art and literature, humans have intermittently celebrated, demonized and humanized cacti as a means of getting to grips with them. With so many conflicting features (and, as a result, so many conflicting interpretations by humans), we seem continually to question what cacti are. And cacti appear to question what they are themselves; why else would they be so keen to hybrid-ize between genera and mutate so dramatically and so easily? Because of this, we appear very happy to change them further, and into something else – perhaps as a means of finally understanding them. And if not, we will at least have had a hand in creating some really spectacular living sculpture.

seven
Cactus Collectors
and Cactus Societies

Most people think of collectibles as being, perhaps, tin toys, porcelain figures or antique vases – seldom cacti. But these plants are highly collectible items, and people have in fact been collecting them for centuries. Cacti are, of course, living organisms; yet, because of their design, unusual form and slow growth, many people are compelled to equate them more with objects than with organisms. A cactus can look much more like a carved sculpture than a living entity, and some species can maintain their form, virtually unchanged, for decades. One writer remarked that the European cactus collector

> can go away for a summer holiday without having to worry that his specimens will become too dry and he can also see them through the winter without undue difficulty, since cacti are not watered during this period and may even be stored wrapped in paper and placed in a drawer in a dry, cold room.[1]

There are certainly not many living things, excluding seeds and bulbs, that one could wrap up in paper and leave in a drawer over the winter. And although this treatment might not be advisable for most cacti, it does illustrate their uniqueness.

Many cactus specimens, even when established, are extremely compact in size – similar to any collectible trinket that one might

Cacti collection, Frankfurt, *c.* 1905.

Jean-Léon Gérôme, *Portrait of a Cactus Collector*, 1853, oil on canvas.

place in a display cabinet. A substantial collection of small ornamental cacti could be housed on a windowsill, or, conceivably, several hundred cacti might fit on a small table. With approximately 1,500 unique species in the cactus family, plus countless hybrids, mutations and variations, there are a lot of cacti for the collector to collect.

Most people who identify themselves as collectors of cacti tend also to be collectors of other things. In her text on the general topic of collecting and collectibles, Claudia Chan-Shaw notes:

The world is made up of collectors and non-collectors. Some people need to collect, others do not. Collecting gives the collector control, the parameters established are limited only by themselves: they make the decisions such as if they should specialize, or if they are going for quality or quantity. For some there is a great satisfaction in arranging, re-arranging, collating, cataloguing, displaying and establishing order. Collectors are defined by their collections and one person's definition of what is precious will be different to another's.[2]

Collectors have been known to amass just about anything, but within the plant kingdom it is cacti that seem to attract them most. Regardless of the subject matter, collectors tend to seek out that which is rare or obscure. Cacti are often viewed as being unconventional, quirky or even unique – which is precisely what makes them so appealing to the collector.

In 1853 the artist Jean-Léon Gérôme painted *Portrait of a Cactus Collector*, which depicts a gentleman seated at a desk next to a small potted cactus. The gentleman appears refined and well-educated; as a 'collector', one would assume him to be a specialist in fine art or antiquities rather than plants. The term 'collector' also conjures images of masses of accumulated objects, but instead of being surrounded by a large assortment of cacti he is accompanied by a single choice specimen. It is as though he is asserting himself as a collector who seeks quality and rarity in the objects he procures.

There are different types of collector: those who seem to hoard nearly every specimen they can get their hands on; and those who might search patiently for a few select, carefully curated, items. Some devote enormous amounts of time and money to the search for a particular specimen, as Chan-Shaw explains: 'A collector is a bit like a compulsive gambler, thrilled by the pursuit, the whole process of the hunt, and then the final possession and sense of accomplishment. Acquisition is such a sweet victory.'[3] Some cactus collectors might focus on plants that are native to Brazil or Chile, or those that belong to the genus *Ariocarpus*, or particular varieties of epiphytic cactus, or perhaps only cristate and monstrose cacti. Others delight in the ordering of their cacti, perhaps arranging them in terms of genera and species, by physical characteristic (hairy cacti, epiphytic cacti, columnar cacti or globular cacti) or by place of origin (Mexico, Peru, Texas, Cuba). Some take this location information to extremes, noting the precise coordinates of where the species can be found in its habitat. Those who live in an appropriate climate might also have outdoor gardens dedicated to cacti, which may include some of the larger columnar or tree-like specimens.

There have been a number of trends in cactus collecting. The old man cactus (*Cephalocereus senilis*) was very popular in the early twentieth century, and seemed to invigorate the cactus-collecting world, attracting many new people to the plants. Its popularity eventually waned, only to be revived several decades later. Currently there seems to be a great deal of interest in exotic cultivars and mutations, and, rather than being shunned for their abnormalities, these plants are now embraced for their extraordinary traits. As one collector has noted, 'A monstrose or cristate plant is a great collector's item because there is only one exactly like it, anywhere.'[4]

It is very easy for the collector of cacti to go from owning just a few dozen to having thousands of individual cactus plants. Many have started by gathering one or two specific varieties, but have soon become enamoured with related species, and then with species related to those. The collectors not only tend to acquire new specimens, but their existing specimens tend to multiply as well. Looking at this from a rather optimistic perspective, one collector has noted:

> The one thing that a cactus collector should remember is that each plant in his collection becomes more valuable to himself or to a potential buyer with each passing year, and if it doesn't die, increases in value just like other kinds of invest-

Card depicting a variety of cacti, c. 1907.

ments, about ten percent per year. This does not take into account that many plants will reproduce themselves with pups which can double and redouble your plant numbers year after year. Nor does it take into account that seeds from your plants can be planted and the number of plants can be increased by the thousands.[5]

However, it is important to bear in mind that caring for cacti can take a lot of work – and that is where the comparison between the collection of ceramic figurines and that of cacti diverges. Nearly universal advice from growers of cacti is that one should never acquire more plants than one could properly look after.

Growing Cacti

Even though some cacti might seem more like objects than plants, they are of course living things that require special care. The cactus family is very diverse, and each variety has equally diverse cultivation requirements. Some grow very slowly, others extremely fast. Some can endure quite cold climates; many cannot. Over time, cactus enthusiasts normally develop their own specialized horticultural methods, but there are a few generalized points to keep in mind.

Drainage is most important: the soil must be very porous, and generally a mixture that is half-and-half potting soil and porous material (such as very coarse sand) is recommended. For the smaller, slower-growing cacti native to very arid conditions, particularly those with tuberous roots, the amount of porous material is often increased – even to 100 per cent. (This more extreme approach is not generally recommended for most cacti, however.) Fast-growing columnar cacti and most epiphytic varieties will appreciate a greater proportion of soil in the mix.[6]

Cacti should be watered more heavily during their growing season, which is generally spring to late summer, but the soil should be allowed to dry out thoroughly between waterings. Most of the smaller and slower-growing cacti are accustomed to dry climates and should not receive much, if any, water in winter. Some of the faster-growing columnar and epiphytic cacti need more water, and will do well even in winter with some watering (or rainfall). However, the metabolism of a cactus generally stops working at about 10°C (50°F), and since their roots cannot readily absorb water in cold weather, rotting can result from over-watering.[7]

Most cacti like a warm and sunny environment. Some do well in full sun, others need partial shade, but all like good light. Many desert cacti appreciate direct sunlight, but all cacti are prone to sunburn and stress, especially if they are not acclimatized. New plants, in particular, should at first have only limited exposure to direct sun.

In Arizona, because of population growth, increasing industrial development and ongoing construction projects, many of the iconic saguaro cacti have been relocated. Unfortunately, quite a few of these transplanted cacti do not survive. Although they may look fine for the first year or two, many expire slowly from the shock of the transplant. To help prevent this, the city of Scottsdale issued a number of guidelines for transplanting, and these are relevant to the removal and relocation of most species of cactus. Among them are:

- Dig around saguaro leaving a minimum of 2 feet [60 cm] of root from the base and deep enough to allow for removal of a reasonable portion of the root ball.
- Saguaro should be re-planted at the same depth or no more than 6 inches [15 cm] deeper than its original position.
- Mark the original north orientation so saguaro may be re-planted in the same direction to reduce risk of sunburn.
- Pack thoroughly, using a mixture of native soil and sandy soil to promote root growth and better drainage.
- After transplant, allow 2–3 weeks for damaged roots to heal before the first watering.
- Saguaro is established once it responds to rainfall by expanding.[8]

Because most cacti come from arid regions and live in very porous soil, they can be prone to fungal infections in damper and colder climates, or if over-watered. A fungus infection usually begins at the base of the plant, at the top of the roots. Any infected plant should immediately be isolated from other cacti. Quite often fungicides fail to kill off an advanced infection, and the best solution in that case is to cut off the plant high on the stem, well into the healthy area, and re-propagate from that section, discarding the rest of the plant.[9] When repotting, brand new or sterilized pots are recommended, as is fresh potting mixture, which will help to prevent the spread of fungi.

Two very common pests that are likely to affect most growers of cacti are mealy bugs and scale insects. Mealy bugs are small, white insects (usually 1–3 mm/⅛ in. long) that like to hide between the ribs, under spines or among the roots of the cacti. They often form a waxy white coating over themselves as protection and, in the same way as aphids, they feed off the plant by sucking its juices. They will not kill the plant immediately, but they can spread quickly, so at the first sign of them a plant should be isolated. Manual treatment, although tedious, can help to keep them at bay: simply squashing the bugs with a finger or toothpick is adequate, but better still is a cotton swab or small paintbrush dipped in alcohol (or methylated spirits). Scale insects appear on the stems as small brown bumps, under which they live and lay their eggs. Once the brown spot is scraped off, the area can be cleaned with alcohol.[10] Most infestations come from introduced plants, such as those newly acquired from other collections, so all new plants should be immediately repotted (checking carefully among the roots for any sign of pest or rot) and isolated for a couple of weeks. During the isolation period the plant should be checked repeatedly and treated if necessary.

There are two kinds of pesticide, topical and systemic. Topical ones work by killing the pests on contact, whereas systemic ones are absorbed by the roots and taken up through the plant, poisoning the pests as they attempt to feed off it. Because pesticides can be extremely dangerous to plant, human and animal health and the environment, most growers have become very cautious about the frequency and manner of using them. Many have switched to primarily organic methods, such as the manual removal of pests and washing plants with soapy mixtures.

Industrial facility for the commercial growing of cacti.

Although insects can be a big problem, many growers have suffered more damage from mammals – opossums, mice and, in particular, rats. One cactus grower has lamented:

> Why is it when a rat or mouse finds his, or her, way into your cactus house it always seems to hunt and find the cactus plant that you would least like to have attacked? On one occasion, the largest and handsomest *Astrophytum myriostigma* var. 'Nudum' that I owned, a beautiful twelve inch high specimen, with dark green body color, was attacked and the whole top eaten out. I have refused to discard this plant, and each time I look at it, it reminds me to watch out for holes or places where a rat might enter.[11]

There are numerous accounts of how rats have ravaged commercial nurseries and large cactus collections. Since rats, in particular, tend to take just a large bite or two out of a plant before moving onto the next, a mere handful of them might destroy the saleability of hundreds of cacti in a single night.

One wonderful thing about cacti is that they are very easy to propagate vegetatively; there are just a few simple guidelines that one should follow. Normally, the cuttings should be taken during the growing season. If the plant is segmented or has produced offsets, these can simply be broken or cut at the joint. If the plant comprises only a single stem, a segment can be cut off it, making sure that the knife is clean and sharp – and not serrated. Once removed, the cutting should be allowed to callus over for a minimum of two weeks; usually several weeks will be needed. The cutting can then be placed upright into porous soil, but it should not be watered for perhaps another couple of weeks. In this way, one can very quickly make multiple copies of a specimen.

Dealing in Cacti

Some collectors of cacti end up becoming part-time dealers, perhaps selling to other cactus enthusiasts at local cactus societies and clubs, or via the Internet, since the compact nature of many cacti makes shipping quite feasible. However, the bulk of cultivated cacti are produced by mid- to large-scale wholesale nurseries. What is often regarded as the first, and is certainly the longest-running, commercial seller of cacti is Kakteen-Haage in Erfurt, Germany, which began in 1822 and is still in operation. A number of other European nurseries had emerged by the mid-nineteenth century, and in Paris, for example, there was a very popular nursery dedicated exclusively to the sale of cacti and succulents. This nursery, under the proprietorship of Monsieur Steiner, was featured in a lengthy magazine article in *Magasin pittoresque* from 1857.

The first American nursery dedicated to cacti was A. Blanc & Co., which was founded in the late nineteenth century by Albert Blanc, an immigrant from Belgium. Soon after arriving in the United States in the 1870s, Blanc opened a small cactus nursery in Philadelphia. In 1886 he published his first mail-order catalogue, and by the 1890s his company had become the world's largest seller of cacti, shipping cacti to nearly every part of the globe.[12] The catalogues produced by the firm listed nearly 500 different species and were illustrated profusely by Blanc himself. In the catalogue of 1892 he made the rather bold statement:

> We claim the entire credit for making Cacti once more popular. This is due greatly to the fact that they are so easy to manage, and so interesting, and also to the fact that at great cost and trouble we have been able to offer to our customers the largest and finest collection in the United States.[13]

Soon competing American cactus nurseries were also offering international distribution, including Lyon & Cobbe of Los Angeles; the

William Tell Cacti Nursery of Austin, Texas; the Callander Cactus Company of Springfield, Ohio; and the Mrs Anna B. Nickels Cactus Nursery of Laredo, Texas (founded by the era's most prominent female collector and dealer of cacti).

All these companies appear to have been fairly successful, selling hundreds of thousands of cacti each year and greatly facilitating the spread of collectible cacti around the world. In 1891 Mikhail Mikhailovich Cantacuzène, Count Speransky, of Russia wrote a letter praising Blanc after receiving an order of cactus plants from America:

> I have just received the cacti ordered of you. The plants arrived in excellent condition, which is remarkable, owing to the long voyage. Only one plant in the entire collection was dead, and that one apparently of a tender nature. I beg to thank you for the fine collection of beautiful specimens. You may expect more orders in the near future.[14]

Although some of the cacti featured in these catalogues were likely to have been collected in the field, as the demand for cacti grew, the majority would have been cultivated from seed or cuttings. Lyon & Cobbe asserted that 'We send none but healthy, good plants; being home-grown they are mostly larger and in better condition than those usually supplied.'[15] Prices ranged considerably, according to species. As an indication, the Lyon & Cobbe catalogue of 1894 offered inexpensive wholesale lots of 100 established peyote cactus plants (*Lophophora williamsii*, then referred to as *Anhalonium williamsii*) for only $15. More expensive plants were sold individually: a 50-cm-tall (20-in.) cardón (*Pachycereus*) and a large bishop's cap (*Astrophytum myriostigma*) went for $5 each, and a large queen of the night, *Cereus grandiflorus* (syn. *Selenicereus grandiflorus*), sold for $10. Around the same time, Luther Burbank was selling his spineless *Opuntia* (prickly pear) for $5 a plant.

In more recent years the international trade in cacti has reached massive proportions. In addition to the Americas and Europe, a

Commercial growing of cacti.

number of Asian countries have become major exporters of cultivated cacti, particularly Japan, Korea and Thailand. Cacti tend to be
robust, and so – as was demonstrated in the nineteenth century –
they are well suited to international trade and can usually withstand
fairly long periods of shipping and storage.

Although many cacti can tolerate quite harsh conditions, they
do not do well with sudden change. Thus, cacti that are grown from
seedlings in a climate-controlled hothouse and then immediately
shipped to nurseries for sale are unlikely to do well. To safeguard
against climate shock, good growers take great care to acclimatize the
plants before selling them. When the cacti have grown to an adequate
size, they are moved to less controlled conditions in order to 'harden'
them off, so that when they are taken home by the customer, they have
a much better chance not only of survival, but of flourishing.

There are various different markets and constantly evolving
trends in the cactus trade. The large 'big box' and chain stores tend
to stock quantities of the common, easy-to-grow ornamental varieties. To supply these markets, growers produce such plants en masse
– by the thousand or sometimes hundreds of thousands – so that the
retailers can offer a consistent product. The popular lollipop cacti are
primarily produced, in their millions, by just a few mega-nurseries in
Korea, Thailand and China; most wholesalers buy from these, then
sell on to other nurseries and retailers.

There is a growing market of speciality collectors, and it is generally the smaller growers who are able to offer varieties that the very large-scale production houses cannot. Smaller, more niche growers have also tapped into the rising trends of monstrose, crested and variegated cacti, which can fetch enormous prices. In more arid climates, as concern about water shortages increases, there has been a definite shift towards 'xeriscaping', landscaping with xerophytic plants that require little or no irrigation. In these regions very large, established, usually locally grown specimens are popular, such as large golden barrels or saguaros; larger specimens also tend to fetch enormous prices.

Protecting Cacti

Many species of cactus are considered to be under threat in their natural environment. Their numbers have been steadily decreasing in the wild, primarily owing to the destruction of habitat – mostly from agricultural development, but also from urbanization and road-building.[16] Thousands of hectares of prime cactus habitat are lost every year, particularly in Mexico and the southwestern United States, and millions of hectares have been cleared and planted with non-native buffelgrass (*Pennisetum ciliare*) for grazing cattle. This not only destroys the growing cacti but greatly increases the risk of wildfires in the region.[17] As the human population continues to grow, the once-overlooked desert regions are now increasingly being seen as economically viable development sites. Social scientist and cacti expert David Yetman has described how not only have these prime cactus habitats been converted to traditional agricultural land for farming, but thousands of acres have been cleared to make way for enormous prawn farms – built where great stands of coastal cacti once grew.[18]

Another threat, albeit a lesser one than the massive loss of habitat, has come from the illegal harvesting of cacti for private collections and commercial wholesale. Even though an increasing number of species are readily available through artificial propagation, it has been suggested that

> Some collectors are like 'stamp collectors' in that they want as many 'originals' as possible, meaning that the plants must come directly from the wild. Thus, uncommon and unusual cacti are frequently the victims of these unscrupulous collectors, who flout local and national laws to satisfy their personal needs.[19]

One mechanism to help stem this trend has been through the creation of CITES, the Convention on International Trade in Endangered Species of Wild Flora and Fauna, a major international treaty that aims to protect endangered flora and fauna, including threatened and endangered cacti. The treaty, which has now been signed by more than 130 countries, maintains a list of all internationally protected specimens, divided into different categories. Species that are listed in Appendix I are heavily protected and described as being at serious risk from commercial trade. There are close to fifty species of cactus listed in Appendix I, and international trade of these field-collected specimens is totally banned, although artificially propagated specimens are allowed with the appropriate permits. Nearly all other species of cactus are listed in Appendix II, indicating that the international trade of field-collected specimens is very strictly regulated.[20] There are only a very few cacti that are not listed in these two categories: some artificially propagated specimens, such as *Schlumbergera* cultivars (Christmas cactus), *Gymnocalycium mihanovichii* (lollipop cacti), which lack chlorophyll, and some commercially grown prickly pear.[21]

Although CITES has helped to prevent the illegal international trade in field-collected cacti, it is left to local legislation and conservation efforts to prevent the continued destruction of habitat and ultimately to ensure the continued survival of threatened species. The two main approaches to cactus conservation are referred to as 'in situ', the protection of cacti in their native habitat (arguably the most effective); and 'ex situ', the cultivation of cacti away from their habitat, in botanic gardens or private collections. A number of conservationists have cautioned that relying purely on the latter method will have a negative long-term effect on the genetic variability of the plants.[22] It has also been argued that nature is usually much better at caring for cacti then many growers are. For example, one author related how a rare find of nearly fifty specimens of *Mammillaria wrightii* were once found in New Mexico, and the discoverer

> promptly took them all, explaining his action by saying that he believed those were all that existed and he felt bound to take every one in order to preserve the species. I think no better criticism of this sort of wholesale gathering of rare plants need be made than to note that not one of his collected plants or any of their offspring can be traced today, but that there have been a few specimens collected in the wild in the years since then, proving that nature is the best preserver of her children after all.[23]

A number of areas in the Americas have been set aside to protect the habitat of cacti, and in the Sonoran Desert there are two federally protected areas specifically for the conservation of two unique species: Organ Pipe Cactus National Monument and Saguaro National Park. There are also several other protected areas in the United States that are rich in cacti, and a number of national parks and preserves have been created in Mexico and some South American countries that secure natural habitats.[24]

In Arizona, nearly all native varieties of cactus are strongly protected by local legislation. If a cactus is on the protected list, it cannot be removed from any property without a permit first being obtained from the Department of Agriculture. Separate permission must be obtained for each listed plant that is to be moved. A permit tag is then placed on the plant before it is dug up, and must remain on the cactus until it is replanted in its new location.

Cactus display in the manner of a chessboard, including a few
Euphorbia succulents. Designed by Peri Jeffrey.

Because of the continued theft and destruction of saguaro cacti,
particularly on protected land, officials have recently begun inserting
tiny microchip radio-frequency identification tags into the cactus
trunks. The tag is about the thickness and shape of a 1-cm-long (½
in.) pencil lead, and can be read electronically when a scanner is held
up to the cactus. The tags are punched deep into the flesh of the
cactus using a small hand-held implant gun, making their removal
impossible. The electronic tags allow the plant to be identified, and
can help in tracking it down if it is stolen.[25] Interestingly, the crested
saguaro (*Carnegiea gigantea* f. *cristate*) has been listed as a Highly Safe-
guarded Protected Native Plant, while the non-cristate saguaros
are less protected, being listed merely as Salvage Restricted Protected
Native Plants.

Most conservationists agree that it is essential to think holis-
tically about the conservation of cacti and that averting the direct
destruction of a plant should be only part of the strategy. For example,
saguaro seedlings normally survive only if they happen to sprout in
the shade of another plant. These 'nurse plants' – usually mesquite,

ironwood and palo verde trees – are crucial in protecting the vulnerable young cacti for the first several years. When these other species are destroyed, the cacti suffer correspondingly. Many pollinators, such as birds and bats, are also linked to the survival of cacti: if these populations sink, so will the cacti, and vice versa.[26]

However, there are many instances in which ex situ conservation is the only option, and some significant and very vital conservation work has been achieved by botanical organizations, most notably the Huntington Botanical Gardens in San Marino, California, and the Royal Botanic Gardens at Kew. Even private collections maintained by hobbyists have been deemed essential to the preservation of cactus species, and the International Organization for Succulent Plant Study has catalogued a number of these collections in its listing of Important Generic Reserve Collections.[27]

Cactus Societies

Towards the end of the nineteenth century and in the early twentieth, as interest in cacti began to grow, a number of cactus societies sprang up all over the world. The German society was formed in Berlin in 1892; the Cactus and Succulent Society of Australia in Melbourne in 1927; the national Cactus and Succulent Society of America in Los Angeles in 1929; and the Cactus and Succulent Society of Great Britain in London in 1932. Most cactus societies are actually cactus *and* succulent societies, since those who appreciate one of these plant groups tend also to appreciate the other. A number of members, though, claim a bias towards cacti, and often consider them to be a very distinctive (but expansive) sub-group within the succulent world. On the other hand, there are some societies that focus on a single genus of cactus, such as the Mammillaria Society in the United Kingdom. There are now cactus societies in dozens of countries across the world. In some countries, such as the U.S. and the UK, such organizations are structured as a larger, national society made up of a number of local affiliates. In other countries a more informal approach is taken, with numerous independent societies spread across the country that are only casually associated.

People join established cactus societies for a wide range of reasons, but surveys have shown that most do so in order to gain access to plants that cannot be purchased at the local nursery, to learn more about cacti, and to meet people who share a similar interest.[28] Members range from highly specialized botanists to hobbyists who simply like 'cacti and succulents'.

Societies hold regular meetings that feature guest speakers, plant sales and exhibits. Larger societies also hold annual or biennial conferences that spotlight internationally recognized keynote speakers as well as a number of other national and international presenters. Such conferences also incorporate exhibitions, workshops, plant sales and excursions to significant gardens and collections.

Each year, societies will hold cactus and succulent shows and competitions, which help to foster excellence in the growing and presenting of spectacular plant specimens. These competitions also serve to educate the public about cacti and attract new members.[29] Most competitions are divided by plant category as well as level of experience, so that more veteran growers can compete in the 'open' categories, and those who are less seasoned as 'novices'.

Historically, cactus competitions have more or less followed the following guidelines:

> Forty per cent of the points should be awarded for cultivation, twenty per cent for rarity, twenty per cent for difficulty, and twenty percent [sic] for trueness to type, that is, what the plant looks like in its natural habitat.[30]

Many plant competitions have evolved over the years, however, and greater emphasis is now placed on artistic creativity and innovation. Competitions today focus less on the presentation of perfect specimens impeccably centred in inconspicuous pots, and rather encompass creative 'staging' and the integrated design of both the plant and the pot. These changes have certainly allowed competitors to be more creative and have resonated well with the viewing public. Cacti, perhaps more than any other plants, can be transformed creatively and manipulated to a great extent, and their amorphous identity and dramatic variations allow an unlimited degree of imagination and artistic design.

Another important role of these societies, particularly in recent decades, has been to facilitate the conservation, cultivation and scientific study of cacti. In particular, the British Cactus and Succulent Society has continually supported both research and conservation projects on a global scale. These efforts have included rescuing cactus plants from development sites, reseeding and replanting cacti in habitat, undertaking field studies and carrying out detailed research into threatened cactus populations. The Cactus and Succulent Society of America has also been very involved in large-scale conservation efforts; one local affiliate, the Tucson Cactus and Succulent Society, has been involved particularly in salvage operations that involve the rescuing of cacti. In their first fifteen years of engagement, its members rescued well in excess of 70,000 cactus plants from destruction arising from new development sites.[31] Even though these operations cannot save the habitat of the cacti, they have saved a remarkable number of plants, contributing to the maintenance of genetic diversity and helping to ensure the long-term survival of the species. Many other societies have worked extensively with local botanic gardens and conservation groups; the Melbourne-based Cactus and Succulent Society of Australia, for example, helped with the re-establishment of the cactus garden at the Royal Botanic Gardens in that city after vandals ruthlessly destroyed it.

In recent years the Internet has greatly expanded the popularity of cacti. Many cactus societies now have a strong online presence, and many other forums and networks have sprung up to allow people to showcase their cactus collections, buy and sell plants, provide growing tips and post images requesting help in the identification or care of particular specimens.

Display plant for competition from the Gates Cactus and Succulent
Society Show, California.

Cactus Futures

Humans have always approached the cactus in novel ways, and we
have been expansive in our contemplation of it. Yet the cactus itself
continues to evolve – both biologically and conceptually – and as it
has changed it has become increasingly accessible and popular. In
parallel, our portrayal of the cactus in art and popular culture has also
broadened. Perhaps a fitting way to conclude is to borrow an extract
from John Thornber and Frances Bonker's book *The Fantastic Clan*
(1932):

> The desert cacti are so different and so beautiful, with their
> symmetry of filigree and lacework, their fantastic shapes and
> marvelous colorings, and in many cases with a perfection of
> design that seems to have just come from the draughting
> board.[32]

Perhaps this freshly 'designed' quality of the cactus is one of the sources of the enduring novelty that animates our perception of it from one era to the next. It will be interesting to see what the future holds, where the cactus is heading and into what it might metamorphose next.

Competition plant from the Gates Cactus and Succulent Society Show, California.

Timeline

c. 65 million years ago	Dinosaurs become extinct
c. 30 million years ago	Cacti begin to arise on the South American continent
c. 5 million years ago	The land masses of North and South America merge, and cacti spread into North America
c. 12,000 years ago	Images of cacti are created on cave walls in the mountains of Peru and Brazil
1300 BC	Cactus artefacts, including a large engraved stone that features a tribute to the San Pedro cactus, are created for the temple of Chavín, Peru
AD 1–800	The Moche culture of Peru; a large number of pottery items depicting cacti have survived from this time
1325	The Aztecs are said to see the prophetic sign of an eagle on a cactus, and establish the capital city of their empire in that spot
1490s	Europeans first encounter cacti in the Caribbean islands
1519	Spanish explorers encounter the production of cochineal dye in Mexico
1520s	The Spanish begin to export cochineal dye from the Americas to Europe

1535	Gonzalo Fernández de Oviedo y Valdés begins publishing what are regarded to be the first printed images of cacti in his *Historia general y natural de las Indias*
1570s	The prickly pear cactus is introduced into Italy; in the 1580s it is brought to England, Germany and France, and in 1610 it is introduced into North Africa
1716	Publication of *Historia plantarum succulentarum* (History of Succulent Plants) by Richard Bradley, featuring a number of detailed images of cacti
1787	*Curtis's Botanical Magazine* commences publication; its founding editor is William Curtis. It contains many articles and illustrations featuring cacti. Cacti are introduced into Australia with the intention of establishing a British cochineal industry there
1822	The Kakteen-Haage nursery (devoted to cacti and succulents) opens in Erfurt, Germany; it is still in operation today
1850	The German painter Carl Spitzweg creates the now celebrated oil painting *The Cactus Enthusiast*
1860s	The French introduce the cultivation of dragon fruit to Vietnam
1870s	The prickly pear cactus is recognized as a pest and invasive weed in Australia. The Belgium migrant Albert Blanc opens the first commercial cactus nursery in the United States
1889	The Baltimore Cactus Society is formed
1890s	Luther Burbank begins work on cultivating his famous 'spineless' prickly pear cactus
1892	The German cactus and succulent society, Deutsche Kakteen-Gesellschaft e.V., is formed
c. 1900	The cactus and succulent garden of the Huntington Botanical Gardens in San Marino, California, is established

1900	The prickly pear 'pest' spreads over vast areas of prime agricultural and grazing land in Australia
1919–23	Nathaniel Britton and Joseph Nelson Rose publish their groundbreaking, comprehensive four-volume study *The Cactaceae*
1925	The first shipment of nearly 3,000 larvae of *Cactoblastis cactorum* moths travels from Argentina to Australia to combat the prickly pear invasion
1927	The Australian Cactus and Succulent Society (Melbourne) is formed
1929	The nationwide Cactus and Succulent Society of America is formed (some local societies are started before and after this date)
1930s	Eiji Watanabe begins developing the 'Hibotan' albino grafted cactus, known as the moon or lollipop cactus
1931	The nationwide British Cactus and Succulent Society is formed (some local societies are started before and after this date)
1932	The Sherman Hoyt Cactus House opens at the Royal Botanic Gardens in Kew, west London
1933	The Saguaro National Monument is established in Arizona. It is elevated to National Park status in 1994
1934	Nearly 90 per cent of the prickly pear infestation in Australia is destroyed, thanks to the introduction of the *Cactoblastis* moth
1937	The Organ Pipe Cactus National Monument is established in Arizona
1940s	The perfumer Howard K. Foncanon launches his original cactus-flower perfumes in Albuquerque, New Mexico
1944	Disney's animated feature film *The Three Caballeros* is released, starring anthropomorphized cacti

1948	The Cactus and Succulent Society of New Zealand is established
1950	The International Organization for Succulent Plant Study (IOS) is established
1951	The Cactus Society of Mexico (Sociedad Mexicana de Cactología) is established
1973	The international treaty CITES (Convention on International Trade in Endangered Species of Wild Fauna and Flora) is created. Most species of cactus are included in the listings
1983	The 'Super Kabuto' cultivar of *Astrophytum asterias* (developed by Masaomi Takeo and Tony Sato) becomes commercially available
1985	The Desert Garden Conservatory is constructed at the Huntington Botanical Gardens
1989	The *Cactoblastis* moth unintentionally spreads to the United States and begins to threaten native cacti in Florida and surrounding states
c. 2000	Dragon fruit become increasingly popular worldwide
2006	The *New Cactus Lexicon* is published. The *Cactoblastis* moth is found on islands off the coast of mainland Mexico, but is quickly eradicated before it can spread to Mexico's substantial prickly pear industry
2008	The Oasis 'Cactus Kid' television advertisements are banned in the United Kingdom

References

Introduction

1 T. S. Eliot, 'The Hollow Men', in *Collected Poems, 1909–1962* (London, 1963), p. 60.
2 Marie D'Alton, 'Origins of the Word "Succulenticon"', in *Proceedings of the 2012 Australian Cactus and Succulent Convention* (Melbourne, 2012), p. 6.

1 Natural History of the Cactus

1 Park S. Nobel, *Desert Wisdom: Agaves and Cacti: co$_2$, Water, Climate Change* (New York, 2010), p. 60.
2 Ibid.
3 James D. Mauseth, Roberto Kiesling and Carlos Ostolaza, *A Cactus Odyssey: Journeys in the Wilds of Bolivia, Peru and Argentina* (Portland, OR, 2002), p. 15.
4 Will Benson, *Kingdom of Plants: A Journey through their Evolution* (London, 2012), p. 183.
5 Edward F. Anderson, *The Cactus Family* (Portland, OR, 2001), p. 38.
6 Ibid.
7 David Hunt, *The New Cactus Lexicon: Illustrations* (Milborne Port, Somerset, 2013).
8 Mauseth, Kiesling and Ostolaza, *A Cactus Odyssey*, p. 5.
9 Ibid., p. 9.
10 Benson, *Kingdom of Plants*, p. 173.
11 Arthur C. Gibson and Park S. Nobel, *The Cactus Primer* (Cambridge, MA, 1986), p. 74.
12 Nobel, *Desert Wisdom*, pp. 145–6.
13 Mauseth, Kiesling and Ostolaza, *A Cactus Odyssey*, p. 10.
14 Gibson and Nobel, *Cactus Primer*, p. 256.
15 Rudolf Schulz and Attila Kapitany, *Copiapoa in their Environment* (Melbourne, 1996), p. 50.
16 Anderson, *Cactus Family*, p. 53
17 Benson, *Kingdom of Plants*, p. 179.

18 Schulz and Kapitany, *Copiapoa*, p. 57.
19 Joseph G. Dubrovsky and Gretchen B. North, 'Root Structure and
    Function', in *Cacti: Biology and Uses*, ed. Park S. Nobel (Los Angeles, CA,
    2002), p. 43.
20 Quoted in Alan Powers, *Nature in Design* (London, 1999), p. 37.
21 Anderson, *Cactus Family*, p. 27.
22 Schulz and Kapitany, *Copiapoa*, p. 60.
23 Anderson, *Cactus Family*, p. 27.
24 Ibid., p. 36.
25 Leo W. Banks, *All About Saguaros: Facts, Lore, Photos* (Phoenix, AZ, 2008),
    p. 41.
26 Anderson, *Cactus Family*, p. 33.
27 David Yetman, *The Great Cacti: Ethnobotany and Biogeography of Columnar
    Cacti* (Tucson, AZ, 2007), p. 42.
28 Benson, *Kingdom of Plants*, pp. 150–51.
29 Banks, *All About Saguaros*, p. 44.
30 Eric Mellink and Mónica E. Riojas-López, 'Consumption of
    Platyopuntias by Wild Vertebrates', in *Cacti: Biology and Uses*,
    ed. Nobel, p. 112.

2 Native Cacti, Alien Cacti

 1 Edward F. Anderson, *The Cactus Family* (Portland, OR, 2001), p. 43.
 2 Gordon Rowley, *A History of Succulents* (Mill Valley, CA, 1997), p. 15.
 3 David Yetman, 'The Cactus Metaphor', in *A Companion to Mexican
    History and Culture*, ed. William H. Beezley (Oxford, 2011), p. 133.
 4 Manuel Aguilar-Moreno, *Handbook to Life in the Aztec World*
    (Los Angeles, CA, 2006), p. 144.
 5 Ibid.
 6 Caroline Dodds Pennock, *Bonds of Blood: Gender, Lifecycle and Sacrifice in
    Aztec Culture* (London, 2008), p. 32.
 7 Maureen Daly Goggin, 'The Extra-ordinary Powers of Red in
    Eighteenth and Nineteenth Century English Needlework', in *The
    Materiality of Color: The Production, Circulation, and Application of Dyes and
    Pigments, 1400–1800*, ed. Andrea Feeser, Maureen Daly Goggin and
    Beth Fowkes Tobin (London, 2012), p. 31.
 8 Amy Butler Greenfield, *A Perfect Red: Empire, Espionage, and the Quest for
    the Color of Desire* (New York, 2005), p. 36.
 9 Ibid., pp. 37–8.
10 Mathew Attokaran, *Natural Food Flavors and Colorants* (Hoboken, NJ,
    2011), p. 307.
11 John James Thornber and Frances Bonker, *The Fantastic Clan:
    The Cactus Family* (New York, 1932), p. 125.
12 R. A. Donkin, *Spanish Red: An Ethnogeographical Study of Cochineal and
    the Opuntia Cactus* (Philadelphia, PA, 1977), p. 40.
13 Ibid., p. 43.

14 W. B. Alexander, *The Prickly Pear in Australia* (Melbourne, 1919), p. 15.
15 Ibid.
16 Australian patent no. 5871, class 30.2, Sydney, 30 July 1912.
17 *Sydney Mail*, 3 January 1912.
18 H. Zimmermann, S. Bloem and H. Klein, *Biology, History, Threat, Surveillance and Control of the Cactus Moth, Cactoblastis cactorum* (Vienna, 2004), pp. 17–18.
19 S. Raghu and Craig Walton, 'Understanding the Ghost of *Cactoblastis* Past: Historical Clarifications on a Poster Child of Classical Biological Control', *BioScience* (2007), pp. 699–705.
20 Zimmermann, Bloem and Klein, *Biology, History, Threat*, p. 21.
21 'Patrol Along a Cactus Curtain', *Life*, LII/17 (1962), p. 2.
22 Jana K. Lipman, *Guantánamo: A Working-class History between Empire and Revolution* (Los Angeles, CA, 2008), p. 166.
23 Thornber and Bonker, *Fantastic Clan*, p. 121.
24 Scott Calhoun, *The Gardener's Guide to Cactus: The 100 Best Paddles, Barrels, Columns, and Globes* (Portland, OR, and London, 2012), p. 125.
25 'Cactus Cattle-guards', *Literary Digest*, 31 January 1914, p. 202.

3 Beautiful Cacti, Beastly Cacti

1 Edward F. Anderson, *The Cactus Family* (Portland, OR, 2001), p. 46.
2 Richard Aitken, *Botanical Riches: Stories of Botanical Exploration* (Melbourne, 2006), p. 83.
3 Gordon Rowley, *A History of Succulents* (Mill Valley, CA, 1997), p. 297.
4 'Works of Art', *Boston Evening Transcript*, 5 December 1855, p. 1, quoted in Amy Ellis, *New Worlds from Old: 19th Century Australian and American Landscapes* (Melbourne, 1998), p. 117.
5 Sergiusz Michalski, *New Objectivity: Painting, Graphic Art and Photography in Weimar Germany, 1919–1933* (London, 2003), p. 165.
6 See www.mariscal.com, accessed 10 October 2014.
7 Amy Youngs, *Interactive Media Exhibition*, exh. cat., Experimenta, Melbourne (2002), p. 23.
8 Richard Brautigan, *Dreaming of Babylon: A Private Eye Novel 1942* (New York, 1977), p. 12.
9 Jan Harold Brunvand, *The Baby Train and Other Lusty Urban Legends* (New York, 1993), pp. 278–82.
10 Roy Vickery, *A Dictionary of Plant-lore* (Oxford, 1995), p. 437.
11 George Thomson, *Melocactus: Care and Cultivation* (Bologna, 2009), p. 5.
12 David Yetman, *The Great Cacti: Ethnobotany and Biogeography of Columnar Cacti* (Tucson, AZ, 2007), p. 70.
13 Arthur Delbridge, ed., *Aussie Talk: The Macquarie Dictionary of Australian Colloquialisms* (Melbourne, 1984), p. 56.
14 Zane Grey, *The Rainbow Trail* (New York, 1915), p. 68.
15 Zane Grey, *Nevada* (New York, 1928), p. 130.

16 Richard Folkard, *Plant Lore, Legends, and Lyrics* (London, 1892), p. 265.
17 E. W. Northnagel, 'He Captured the Desert's Fragrance', *Desert Magazine*, XIX/12 (1956), pp. 9–11.
18 Dr Seuss, *Hop on Pop* (New York, 1963), pp. 30–31.
19 Vincent Cerutti and Paul Starosta, *Cacti* (Berlin, 1998), p. 8. Although not referencing this particular product explicitly, the authors describe that the fibres from these two cacti were most commonly used 'for stuffing pillows and mattresses'.

4 Almost Human: The Anthropomorphic Cactus

1 Paul Wells, *Basics Animation: Scriptwriting* (Lausanne, 2007), pp. 26–7.
2 Andy Coghlan, 'Why Humans Alone have Pubic Hair', *New Scientist*, 27 February 2009, www.newscientist.com.
3 Ibid.
4 Leo W. Banks, *All About Saguaros: Facts, Lore, Photos* (Phoenix, AZ, 2008), p. 19.
5 Reg Manning, *What Kinda Cactus Izzat?* (Phoenix, AZ, 1941), p. 29.
6 A brief paraphrase of the historic legend that is published in Banks, *All About Saguaros*, pp. 89–92.
7 David Yetman, 'The Cactus Metaphor', in *A Companion to Mexican History and Culture*, ed. William H. Beezley (Oxford, 2011), p. 135.
8 *Illustrated London News*, 17 October 1846, p. 245.
9 *Punch*, 25 March 1931, p. 327.
10 Barbara Larson, 'Evolution and Degeneration in the Early Work of Odilon Redon', *Nineteenth-century Art Worldwide*, II/2 (2003), www.19thc-artworldwide.org.
11 Michael Facos, *Symbolist Art in Context* (Berkeley, CA, 2009), p. 31.
12 Jay P. Telotte, *The Mouse Machine: Disney and Technology* (Urbana, IL, 2008), pp. 77–8.
13 Quoted in Banks, *All About Saguaros*, p. 85.
14 'The Green Horror', *Fantastic Fears*, I/8 (1954).
15 'The Monster in Hyde Park', *The Wizard*, 1,384 (1952), p. 136.
16 *West Coast Avengers*, II/17 (1987), p. 13.
17 *Doctor Who: Meglos*, DVD (2011).
18 Brendan O'Neill, 'Spike the ASA, not the Cactus Kid', *The Guardian*, 9 October 2008, www.theguardian.com.
19 See www.tokidoki.it/cactus, 7 July 2014.

5 Eating Cacti

1 'The Cactus Eaters', *Harper's Weekly*, 16 November 1867, p. 733.
2 David Yetman, *The Great Cacti: Ethnobotany and Biogeography of Columnar Cacti* (Tucson, AZ, 2007), p. 66.
3 Ran Knishinsky, *Prickly Pear Cactus Medicine: Treatments for Diabetes, Cholesterol, and the Immune System* (Rochester, NY, 2004), p. 25.

4 Park S. Nobel, *Desert Wisdom: Agaves and Cacti: co₂, Water, Climate Change* (New York, 2010), p. 25.

5 William F. Anderson, *The Cactus Family* (Portland, OR, 2001), p. 54.

6 Nobel, *Desert Wisdom*, p. 13.

7 Paolo Inglese, Filadelfio Basile and Mario Schirra, 'Cactus Pear Fruit Production', in *Cacti: Biology and Uses*, ed. Park S. Nobel (Berkeley, CA, 2002), p. 172.

8 Nobel, *Desert Wisdom*, p. 14.

9 Ibid.

10 Anderson, *Cactus Family*, p. 53.

11 See www.tamborinedragonfruitfarm.com.au, accessed 3 November 2014.

12 Anderson, *Cactus Family*, p. 51.

13 Ibid., p. 56.

14 Knishinsky, *Prickly Pear Cactus Medicine*, p. 27.

15 Anderson, *Cactus Family*, p. 56.

16 Ibid., p. 58.

17 Carmen Sáenz-Hernández, Joel Corrales-García and Gildardo Aquino-Pérez, 'Nopalitos, Mucilage, Fiber, and Cochineal', in *Cacti: Biology and Uses*, ed. Nobel, pp. 217, 219.

18 Knishinsky, *Prickly Pear Cactus Medicine*, p. 21.

19 Ibid.

20 Anderson, *Cactus Family*, p. 56.

21 Ibid., p. 59.

22 Ibid., p. 57.

23 Nicolas de Castro Campos Pinto and Elita Scio, 'The Biological Activities and Chemical Composition of *Pereskia* Species (Cactaceae): A Review', *Plant Foods for Human Nutrition*, 69 (2014), p. 193.

24 Anderson, *Cactus Family*, p. 61.

25 Barbara A. Somervill, *Great Empires of the Past: Empire of the Aztecs* (New York, 2010), p. 129.

26 Scott E. Haselton, *Cacti for the Amateur* (London, 1940), p. 17.

27 *The Sultan Drug Co.* (St Louis, MO, 1892), p. 206.

28 Anderson, *Cactus Family*, p. 47.

29 Ibid., p. 44.

30 Ibid., p. 45.

31 Ibid., p. 44.

32 Ibid., p. 46.

33 Ibid., p. 47.

34 See www.gardenfreedom.com/the-proposed-legislation, accessed 4 March 2011.

35 Ali Nefzaoui and Hichem Ben Salem, 'Forage, Fodder, and Animal Nutrition', in *Cacti: Biology and Uses*, ed. Nobel, p. 207.

36 Nobel, *Desert Wisdom*, p. 19.

37 Nefzaoui and Ben Salem, 'Forage, Fodder, and Animal Nutrition', p. 200.

6 Transforming the Cactus

1 William F. Anderson, *The Cactus Family* (Portland, OR, 2001), p. 95.
2 *Luther Burbank's Spineless Cactus* (San Francisco, CA, 1912), p. 3.
3 Gordon Rowley, *A History of Succulents* (Mill Valley, CA, 1997), p. 160.
4 *Luther Burbank's Spineless Cactus* (San Francisco, CA, 1913), p. 26.
5 Aikichi Kobayashi, 'Cacti and Succulents in Japan. Part 3: Some Cultivars of Astrophytum Asterias and Astrophytum Myriostigma', *Cactus and Succulent Journal*, LXVIII/5 (1996), p. 245.
6 Tim Harvey, 'Succulent Cultivars and Hybrids: An Introduction', *Cactus and Succulent Journal*, LXXXVI/5 (2014), pp. 180–93.
7 Gordon Rowley, *Teratopia: The World of Cristate and Variegated Succulents* (Bologna, 2006), p. 146.
8 Aikichi Kobayashi, 'Cacti and Succulents in Japan. Part 2: Hibotan and Hibotan-Nishiki, Past and Present', *Cactus and Succulent Journal*, LXVIII/I (1996), p. 21.
9 Rowley, *Teratopia*, p. 97.
10 Danny Schuster, *The World of Cacti: How to Select from and Care for Over 1,000 Species* (New York, 1991), p. 47.
11 Rowley, *Teratopia*, p. 99.
12 Harvey, 'Succulent Cultivars and Hybrids', p. 181.
13 Edward V. Bloom, *Collectors' Cacti* (London, 1960), p. 34.
14 Rowley, *Teratopia*, p. 150.
15 David Yetman and Thomas R. Van Devender, *Maya Ethnobotany: Land, History and Traditional Knowledge in Northwest Mexico* (Berkeley, CA, 2002), p. 83.
16 Traude Gomez Rhine, 'A Clean Start: Propagating Rare Plants in the Huntington's Tissue Culture Lab', *Huntington Frontiers* (Autumn/ Winter 2009), p. 23.
17 Philip W. Clayton et al., 'Micropropagation of Members of the Cactaceae Subtribe Cactinae', *Journal of the American Society for Horticultural Science*, CXV/2 (1990), p. 337.
18 See www.thecactusproject.com, accessed 12 July 2014.
19 Paul Lewis, 'The Edge Effect: Art, Science, and Ecology in a Deleuzian Century', in *An (Un)Likely Alliance: Thinking Environment(s) with Deleuze/Guattari*, ed. Bernd Herzogenrath (Newcastle, 2008), p. 285.

7 Cactus Collectors and Cactus Societies

1 Rudolf Subik, *Decorative Cacti: A Guide to Succulent House Plants*, trans. Olga Kuthanova (London, 1971), pp. 6–7.
2 Claudia Chan-Shaw, *Collectomania: From Objects of Desire to Magnificent Obsession* (Sydney, 2012), p. 3.
3 Ibid., p. 4.
4 Ed Maddox, *Hunting Cactus in Texas* (Texas, 1984), p. 40.

5   Ibid., p. 89.
6   Gerhard Gröner and Erich Götz, *Beautiful Cacti: A Basic Grower's Guide*, trans. Elisabeth E. Reinersmann (New York, 1992), p. 31.
7   Ibid., p. 33.
8   'Chapter 10: Native Plants', in City of Scottsdale, *Design Standards & Policies Manual* (Scottsdale, AZ, 2010), p. 7.
9   Gröner and Götz, *Beautiful Cacti*, p. 56.
10 Ibid., p. 57.
11 Maddox, *Hunting Cactus in Texas*, p. 88.
12 Larry Mitich, 'The World of A. Blanc', *Cactus and Succulent Journal*, XLV/4 (1973), pp. 158–70.
13 Albert Blanc, *Illustrated Catalogue of Rare Cacti* (Philadelphia, PA, 1892), p. 1.
14 Quoted ibid., p. 16.
15 Lyon & Cobbe, *Wholesale Price List of Cacti, Agaves and Other Succulents* (Los Angeles, CA, 1894), p. 1.
16 Sara Oldfield, ed., *Cactus and Succulent Plants: Status Survey and Conservation Action Plan* (Cambridge, 1997), p. 20.
17 David Yetman, *The Organ Pipe Cactus* (Tucson, AZ, 2006), p. 55.
18 Ibid., p. 56.
19 Thomas H. Boyle and Edward F. Anderson, 'Biodiversity and Conservation', in *Cacti: Biology and Uses*, ed. Park S. Nobel (Berkeley, CA, 2002), p. 131.
20 Oldfield, *Cactus and Succulent Plants*, p. 31.
21 David Hunt, ed., *CITES Cactaceae Checklist*, 2nd edn (London, 1999), p. 14.
22 Edward F. Anderson, *The Cactus Family* (Portland, OR, 2001), p. 80.
23 Del Weniger, *Cacti of the Southwest: Texas, New Mexico, Oklahoma, Arkansas, and Louisiana* (Austin, TX, 1970), p. 151.
24 Anderson, *Cactus Family*, p. 79.
25 Jim Burnett, 'Saguaro National Park Using New Technology to Deter Cactus Rustlers', March 2012, www.nationalparkstraveler.com.
26 Rose Houk, *Wild Cacti* (New York, 1996), p. 108.
27 Anderson, *Cactus Family*, p. 82.
28 Attila Kapitany, communication with the author, 2 June 2015.
29 Ibid.
30 R. Ginns, *Cacti and Other Succulents* (London, 1963), p. 62.
31 Joe and Patsy Frannea, 'Saving Cactus, a Priority for TCSS', *Desert Breeze: Newsletter of the Tucson Cactus and Succulent Society* (January 2012).
32 John James Thornber and Frances Bonker, *The Fantastic Clan: The Cactus Family* (New York, 1932), p. vii.

Further Reading

Anderson, Edward F., *The Cactus Family* (Portland, OR, 2001)
Banks, Leo W., *All About Saguaros: Facts, Lore, Photos* (Phoenix, AZ, 2008)
Calhoun, Scott, *The Gardener's Guide to Cactus: The 100 Best Paddles, Barrels, Columns, and Globes* (Portland, OR, and London, 2012)
Gibson, Arthur C., and Park S. Nobel, *The Cactus Primer* (Cambridge, MA, 1986)
Greenfield, Amy Butler, *A Perfect Red: Empire, Espionage, and the Quest for the Color of Desire* (New York, 2005)
Gröner, Gerhard, and Erich Götz, *Beautiful Cacti: A Basic Grower's Guide*, trans. Elisabeth E. Reinersmann (New York, 1992)
Hunt, David, *The New Cactus Lexicon: Illustrations* (Milborne Port, Somerset, 2013)
Kapitany, Attila, and Rudolf Schulz, *Succulents: Propagation* (Melbourne, 2004)
Knishinsky, Ran, *Prickly Pear Cactus Medicine: Treatments for Diabetes, Cholesterol, and the Immune System* (Rochester, NY, 2004)
Mauseth, James D., Roberto Kiesling and Carlos Ostolaza, *A Cactus Odyssey: Journeys in the Wilds of Bolivia, Peru and Argentina* (Portland, OR, 2002)
Nobel, Park S., *Desert Wisdom: Agaves and Cacti: CO_2, Water, Climate Change* (New York, 2010)
—, ed., *Cacti: Biology and Uses* (Los Angeles, CA, 2002)
Rowley, Gordon, *A History of Succulents* (Mill Valley, CA, 1997)
—, *Teratopia: The World of Cristate and Variegated Succulents* (Bologna, 2006)
Schulz, Rudolf, and Attila Kapitany, *Copiapoa in their Environment* (Melbourne, 1996)
Schuster, Danny, *The World of Cacti: How to Select from and Care for Over 1000 Species* (New York, 1990)
Yetman, David, *The Great Cacti: Ethnobotany and Biogeography of Columnar Cacti* (Tucson, AZ, 2007)
—, *The Organ Pipe Cactus* (Tucson, AZ, 2006)
—, and Thomas R. Van Devender, *Maya Ethnobotany: Land, History and Traditional Knowledge in Northwest Mexico* (Berkeley, CA, 2002)

Associations and Websites

General

THE CACTUS AND SUCCULENT PLANT MALL
Provides a vast amount of information on cacti and provides links to virtually
every cactus society in the world.
www.cactus-mall.com

INTERNATIONAL ORGANIZATION FOR SUCCULENT PLANT STUDY
Promotes the worldwide study and conservation of succulent plants.
www.iosweb.org

National and regional societies

THE BRITISH CACTUS AND SUCCULENT SOCIETY
Journal publication and information about the numerous branch societies.
www.bcss.org.uk

CACTUS AND SUCCULENT SOCIETY OF AMERICA
Journal publication and information about the numerous branch societies.
www.cssainc.org

THE CACTUS AND SUCCULENT SOCIETY OF AUSTRALIA
www.cssaustralia.org.au

CACTUS & SUCCULENT SOCIETY OF NEW ZEALAND
www.cssnz.net

THE CACTUS AND SUCCULENT SOCIETY OF NSW
www.cssnsw.org.au

THE CACTUS AND SUCCULENT SOCIETY OF QUEENSLAND
www.cssq.org.au

CACTUS & SUCCULENT SOCIETY OF THE ACT
www.cactusact.org.au

THE CACTUS AND SUCCULENT SOCIETY OF SOUTH AUSTRALIA
www.csssa.org.au

THE CACTUS AND SUCCULENT SOCIETY OF WESTERN AUSTRALIA
www.csswa.org.au

CACTUS SOCIETY OF MEXICO (SOCIEDAD MEXICANA DE CACTOLOGÍA)
www.mexican.cactus-society.org (English website)

Collections of cacti

CACTUS COUNTRY
Victoria, Australia
www.cactuscountry.com.au

DESERT BOTANICAL GARDEN
Phoenix, Arizona
www.dbg.org

THE HUNTINGTON BOTANICAL GARDENS
San Marino, California
www.huntington.org

JARDÍN BOTÁNICO DEL IBUNAM
Mexico
www.ib.unam.mx/jardin/

JARDIN EXOTIQUE DE MONACO
Monaco
www.jardin-exotique.mc

ROYAL BOTANIC GARDENS, KEW
London
www.kew.org

ROYAL BOTANIC GARDENS VICTORIA
Melbourne, Australia
www.rbg.vic.gov.au

THE RUTH BANCROFT GARDEN
Walnut Creek, California
www.ruthbancroftgarden.org

Journals

THE CACTUS EXPLORER
Online journal of the Cactus Explorers Club
www.cactusexplorers.org.uk

XEROPHILIA
English and Romanian
www.xerophilia.ro

Acknowledgements

I would like to thank the members of the Cactus and Succulent Society of Australia, in particular Noelene Tomlinson, Andrew Thompson, Attila Kapitany, Joylene Sutherland and Wayne Robinson. I am grateful to Paradisia Nurseries / Collectors Corner and to Cactus Country of Victoria, Australia, for their assistance with photos and information. I would also like to express my gratitude to Richard Allen and to Phung Allen. Finally, a big thanks to my family for their constant support and to Lienors for reminding me that not everyone likes cacti as much as I do.

Photo Acknowledgements

The author and publishers wish to express their thanks to the following sources for illustrative material and/or permission to reproduce it. Some locations of works are given below rather than in the captions for brevity.

Photo Richard Allen: p. 138 (bottom); photos author: pp. 8, 10 (top), 12, 13, 20, 22–3, 24, 25, 27 (top), 30, 32, 37, 38, 41, 42, 70, 94 (top and bottom), 96, 97, 99, 100, 103, 126 (top and bottom), 130, 134, 139, 140, 142–3, 144, 145, 148, 149, 160–61, 164, 166–7, 170, 171, 174, 184, 188; © 2016 Banco de México Diego Rivera & Frida Kahlo Museums Trust, Av. 5 de Mayo No. 2, Col. Centro, Del. Cuauhtémoc 06059, Mexico City: p. 113; courtesy Laura Cinti and Howard Boland, C-LAB: p. 173; courtesy Lucy Culliton: p. 83; photo Edward S. Curtis/ Library of Congress, Washington, DC (Prints and Photographs Collection – Edward S. Curtis Collection): p. 141; photos Ede Horton: pp. 27 (bottom), 34, 45, 168; photos Attila Kapitany: pp. 192, 196, 197; photo Markus Kellow: p. 102; courtesy Javier Mariscal: p. 84; Metropolitan Museum of Art, bequest of Catherine Vance Gaisman, 2010: p. 133; © Punch Ltd: p. 107; courtesy State Library of Queensland, from the Queenslander Pictorial, supplement to *The Queenslander*, 27 March 1915: p. 61; photo April Torre: p. 44 (bottom); photo Paul Torre: p. 16; courtesy Sharon Weiser: p. 82; courtesy Valentina Gonzalez Wohlers: pp. 85, 93.

Daderot, the copyright holder of the image on p. 73, has published this online under conditions imposed by a Creative Commons CC0 1.0 Universal Public Domain Dedication license; Raquel Baranow, the copyright holder of the image on p. 169, Rob Bertholf, the copyright holder of the image on p. 135, Jean-Guy Dallaire, the copyright holder of the image on p. 43, Amante Darmanin, the copyright holder of the image on p. 28, CC Rogers, the copyright holder of the image on p. 68, and Municipalidad de Antofagasta, the copyright holder of the image on p. 19 have published these online under conditions imposed by a Creative Commons Attribution 2.0 Generic license; BriYYZ, the copyright holder of the image on pp. 66–7, bunky's pickle, the copyright holder of the image on p. 44 (top), and Alan Stark, the copyright holder of the image on p. 18

Index